Real Writing 3

with answers

Roger Gower

CAMBRIDGE
UNIVERSITY PRESS

'CAMBRIDGE
UNIVERSITY PRESS

University Printing House, Cambridge CB2 8BS, United Kingdom

One Liberty Plaza, 20th Floor, New York, NY 10006, USA

477 Williamstown Road, Port Melbourne, VIC 3207, Australia

4843/24, 2nd Floor, Ansari Road, Daryaganj, Delhi – 110002, India

79 Anson Road, #06–04/06, Singapore 079906

Cambridge University Press is part of the University of Cambridge.

It furthers the University's mission by disseminating knowledge in the pursuit of education, learning and research at the highest international levels of excellence.

www.cambridge.org
Information on this title: www.cambridge.org/9780521705929

© Cambridge University Press 2008

First published 2008
Reprinted 2017

Printed in Italy by Rotolito Lombarda S.p.A.

A catalogue record for this publication is available from the British Library

ISBN 978-0-521-70592-9 paperback with answers and audio CD
ISBN 978-0-521-70593-6 paperback without answers

Contents

Map of the book

Unit number	Title	Topic	How to ...
Social and Travel			
1	Are there any rooms free?	Holiday accommodation	○ write to a hotel to get information about services ○ write to find out about accommodation ○ divide an email into well-organized, logically ordered paragraphs ○ write in a suitable style for the situation
2	Thanks and best wishes	Personal communication.	○ write a polite letter of sympathy ○ write a polite but friendly letter of congratulation ○ write in a polite and formal style when necessary ○ write in a polite and friendly style when necessary ○ use a good range of appropriate vocabulary when writing
3	Lost!!!	Renting, selling and trying to find	○ write a short, clear small ad for a noticeboard ○ write a small ad for a newspaper ○ logically structure a small ad ○ use abbreviations in notices ○ use participles in notices
4	Fill in this form, please	Banking, postal and other services	○ understand the headings on an application form ○ complete a form clearly and accurately ○ use the correct spelling on a form ○ use the requested style ○ write figures in words
5	The most amazing place!	Descriptions of places	○ write an email describing a place ○ write a travel blog ○ use adjective phrases to make descriptions vivid ○ use capital letters and punctuation correctly
6	I thought it was great!	Website reviews	○ write an informal review for a website ○ write persuasively ○ use adverb + adjective combinations for personal opinions ○ use linking expressions correctly
Work and Study			
7	Keep it brief	Functioning at work	○ use abbreviations effectively ○ listen and take short, clear notes ○ write simple messages
8	Here's what to do	Instructions and guidelines	○ write instructions saying how something works ○ use imperative forms to give instructions ○ present instructions clearly ○ use sequence words to show the order things happen

Work and Study

Acknowledgements

The author would like to thank the editorial team of Nóirín Burke, Claire Cole, Frances Disken, Ros Henderson, Nicholas Murgatroyd, Caroline Thiriau and Martine Walsh, who have all brought their patience and expertise to bear at various points in the project.

The authors and publishers are grateful for the following reviewers for their valuable insights and suggestions:

Vanessa Boutefeu, UK
Ian Chisholm, UK
Helen Cocking, UK
Stephanie Dimond-Bayir, UK
Helen Dixon, UK
Philip Dover, Cambodia
Jean Greenwood, UK
Sharon Hartle, Italy
Rania Khalil Jabr, Egypt
Hanna Kijowska, Poland
Beatriz Martin, Spain
Marc Sheffner, Japan
Wayne Trotman, Turkey
Tadeusz Z. Womanski, Poland

The authors and publishers acknowledge the following sources of copyright material and are grateful for the permissions granted. While every effort has been made, it has not always been possible to identify the sources of all the material used, or to trace all copyright holders. If any omissions are brought to our notice, we will be happy to include the appropriate acknowledgements on reprinting.

p. 22: section of vehicle licensing form, Crown Copyright, © Driver and Vehicle Licensing Agency, Swansea, SA6 7JL; p. 24: Moneygram form, © Moneygram International; p. 25: section of Post Office insurance form, © Copyright Post Office Ltd 2007; p. 35: Indian visa application form, © Indian Embassy; p. 46: four extracts from *Cambridge Advanced Learner's Dictionary*, *2nd Edition*, 2005 © Cambridge University Press. Reproduced with permission. p. 63: Text A adapted from http://www.filmsite.org/horrorfilms.html, © Tim Dirks; p. 63: Text B based on http://en.wikipedia.org/wiki/Horror_film; p.65: extracts from *The Cambridge Encyclopedia of Language* by David Crystal. Copyright © 1987 David Crystal. Used by permission of Cambridge University Press; p. 76: adapted text from 'Smashing Greek custom goes to the wall', *Sunday Telegraph*, 23 November 2003, © Telegraph Group Ltd; p. 78: text from 'Happiness is … a tiny island in the Pacific' from *The Independent*, © Independent News and Media Limited.

The publishers are grateful to the following for permission to reproduce copyright photographs and material:

Key: l = left, c = centre, r = right, t = top, b = bottom

Alamy/©Bill Bachman for p. 27 /©David South for p. 29; Art Archive/©Musée du Louvre, Paris/Alfredo Dogli Orti for p. 62 (l); Club Med for p. 74; Corbis Images/©Danny Lehman for p. 11/ ©Mango Productions for p. 17 /©Christie's Images for p. 62 (c) /©Alexander Burkatovski for p. 62 (r); Getty Images for pp. 13, 26, 68; Kobal Collection/©Fox 2000/20th Century Fox/Suzanne Tenner for p. 30; Lonely Planet Images/ ©Richard I'Anson for p. 78; Photolibrary/©Image Stock Imagery for p. 10 /©Timothy OKeefe for p. 34 /©Graham Kirk for p. 79; Punchstock/©westend61 for p. 60; Rex for p. 76; Ronald Grant Archive for p. 63; Shutterstock/©Ronen for p. 36 /©Pavel Kapish for p. 41 /©OlgaLis for p. 55.

Illustrations:

Mark Duffin pp. 18, 20, 23, 35, 38, 49, 54c; Kamae Design pp. 56, 70, 71, 72; Katie Mac pp. 40, 54r; Laura Martinez pp. 51, 69; Julian Mosedale pp. 33, 80; Valeryia Steadman pp. 21, 65.

Text design and page make-up: Kamae Design, Oxford
Cover design: Kamae Design, Oxford
Cover photo: © Getty Images
Picture research: Hilary Luckcock

Introduction

To the student

Who is *Real Writing 3* for?

You can use this book if you are a student at intermediate to upper-intermediate level and you want to improve your English writing. You can use the book alone without a teacher or you can use it in a classroom with a teacher.

How will *Real Writing 3* help me with my writing?

Real Writing 3 contains everyday writing practice, for example writing emails and letters and filling in forms. It is designed to help you with writing you will need to do in English at home or when visiting another country.

The exercises in each unit help you develop useful skills such as planning, thinking about the reader and checking your work. There are also activities that help you improve the organization of your writing, your punctuation and your spelling.

How is *Real Writing 3* organized?

The book has 16 units and is divided into two sections:
- Units 1–6 – social and travel situations
- Units 7–16 – work and study situations

Every unit has:
- *Get ready to write*: to introduce you to the topic of the unit
- *Learning tip*: to help you improve your learning
- *Class bonus*: an exercise you can do with other students or friends
- *Focus on*: to help you study useful grammar or vocabulary
- *Did you know?*: extra information about vocabulary, different cultures or the topic of the unit
- *Can-do checklist*: to help you think about what you learnt in the unit

Most units also have:
- *Extra practice*: an extra exercise for more practice

After each section there is a review unit. The reviews help you practise the skills you learn in each section.

At the back of the book you can find:
- *Appendices*: contain lists of *Useful language* for every unit and useful information on punctuation, spelling and linking expressions.
- *Audioscript*: includes everything that you can hear on the audio CD and gives information about the nationalities of the speakers.
- *Answer key*: gives correct answers and possible answers for exercises that have more than one answer.

How can I use *Real Writing 3*?

The units at the end of the book are more difficult than the units at the beginning of the book. However, you do not need to do the units in order. It is better to choose the units that are most interesting for you and to do them in the order you prefer.

There are many different ways you can use this book. We suggest you work in this way:
- Look in the *Contents* list and find a unit that interests you.
- Do the *Get ready to write* section at the start of the unit. This will help you think about the topic of the unit.
- Go to *Appendix 1: Useful language* and look at the wordlist for the unit you want to do. You can use a dictionary to help you understand the words.
- Do the other exercises in the unit in order. At the end of each exercise check your answers with your teacher or in the *Answer key*.
- Try to do the listening exercises without looking at the *Audioscript*. You can read the *Audioscript* after you finish the exercises.
- If your answers are wrong, study the section again to see where you made mistakes.
- After you finish the *Write* exercise, use the *Check* questions to correct your writing.
- If you want to do more work on this topic, do the *Extra practice* activity.
- At the end of the unit, think about what you learnt and complete the *Can-do checklist*.
- Go to *Appendix 1* and look at the *Useful language* for the unit again.

Introduction

To the teacher

What is *Cambridge English Skills*?

Real Writing 3 is one of twelve books in the *Cambridge English Skills* series. The series also contains *Real Reading* and *Real Listening & Speaking* books and offers skills training to students from elementary to advanced level. All the books are available in with-answers and without-answers editions.

Level	Book	Author
Elementary CEF: A2 Cambridge ESOL: KET NQF Skills for life: Entry 2	Real Reading 1 with answers	Liz Driscoll
	Real Reading 1 without answers	Liz Driscoll
	Real Writing 1 with answers and audio CD	Graham Palmer
	Real Writing 1 without answers	Graham Palmer
	Real Listening & Speaking 1 with answers and audio CD	Miles Craven
	Real Listening & Speaking 1 without answers	Miles Craven
Pre-intermediate CEF: B1 Cambridge ESOL: PET NQF Skills for life: Entry 3	Real Reading 2 with answers	Liz Driscoll
	Real Reading 2 without answers	Liz Driscoll
	Real Writing 2 with answers and audio CD	Graham Palmer
	Real Writing 2 without answers	Graham Palmer
	Real Listening & Speaking 2 with answers and audio CD	Sally Logan & Craig Thaine
	Real Listening & Speaking 2 without answers	Sally Logan & Craig Thaine
Intermediate to upper-intermediate CEF: B2 Cambridge ESOL: FCE NQF Skills for life: Level 1	Real Reading 3 with answers	Liz Driscoll
	Real Reading 3 without answers	Liz Driscoll
	Real Writing 3 with answers and audio CD	Roger Gower
	Real Writing 3 without answers	Roger Gower
	Real Listening & Speaking 3 with answers and audio CD	Miles Craven
	Real Listening & Speaking 3 without answers	Miles Craven
Advanced CEF: C1 Cambridge ESOL: CAE NQF Skills for life: Level 2	Real Reading 4 with answers	Liz Driscoll
	Real Reading 4 without answers	Liz Driscoll
	Real Writing 4 with answers and audio CD	Simon Haines
	Real Writing 4 without answers	Simon Haines
	Real Listening & Speaking 4 with answers and audio CD	Miles Craven
	Real Listening & Speaking 4 without answers	Miles Craven

Where are the teacher's notes?

The series is accompanied by a dedicated website containing detailed teaching notes and extension ideas for every unit of every book. Please visit www.cambridge.org/englishskills to access the *Cambridge English Skills* teacher's notes.

What are the main aims of *Real Writing 3*?

- To help students develop writing skills in accordance with the ALTE (Association of Language Testers in Europe) Can-do statements. These statements describe what language users can typically do at different levels and in different contexts. Visit www.alte.org for further information.
- To encourage autonomous learning by focusing on learner training when appropriate.

What are the key features of *Real Writing 3*?

- It is aimed at intermediate to upper-intermediate learners of English at level B2 of the Council of Europe's CEFR (Common European Framework of Reference for Languages).
- It contains 16 four-page units, divided into two sections: Social and Travel, and Work and Study.
- *Real Writing 3* units contain:
  - *Get ready to write* warm-up exercises to get students thinking about the topic
  - *Learning tips* which give students advice on how to improve their writing and their learning
  - *Focus on* activities which provide contextualized practice in particular language areas
  - *Class bonus* communication activities for pairwork and group work so you can adapt the material to suit your class
  - *Did you know?* boxes which provide notes on cultural or linguistic differences between English-speaking countries, or factual information on the topic of the unit
  - *Extra practice* exercises which give students a chance to find out more information about the topic for themselves
  - *Can-do checklists* at the end of every unit to encourage students to think about what they have learnt.
- There are two review units to practise skills that have been introduced in the units.
- It has an international feel and contains a range of native and non-native English accents.
- It can be used as self-study material, in class, or as supplementary homework material.

What is the best way to use *Real Writing 3* in the classroom?

The book is designed so that there is no set way to work through the units. The units may be used in any order, although the more difficult units naturally appear near the end of the book, in the Work and Study section.

You can consult the unit-by-unit teacher's notes at www.cambridge.org/englishskills for detailed teaching ideas. However, broadly speaking, different parts of the book can be approached in the following ways:

- *Useful language*: You can use the *Useful language* lists in the *Appendices* to support the writing activities you are focussing on.
- *Get ready to write*: It is a good idea to use this section as an introduction to the topic. Students can work on the exercises in pairs or groups. Many of these exercises require students to answer questions about their personal experience. These questions can be used as prompts for discussion. Some exercises contain a problem-solving element that students can work on together.
- *Learning tips*: You can ask students to read and discuss these in an open-class situation. An alternative approach is for you to create a series of discussion questions associated with the *Learning tip*. Students can discuss their ideas in pairs or small groups followed by open-class feedback. The *Learning tip* acts as a reflective learning tool to help promote learner autonomy.
- *Class bonuses*: The material in these activities aims to provide freer practice. You can set these up carefully, then take the role of observer during the activity so that students carry out the exercise freely. You can make yourself available to help students or analyze the language they produce during the activity.
- *Extra practice*: These can be set as homework or out-of-class projects for your students. Alternatively, students can do some exercises in pairs during class time.
- *Can-do checklists*: Refer to these at the beginning of a lesson to explain to students what the lesson will cover, and again at the end so that students can evaluate their learning for themselves.
- *Appendices*: You may find it useful to refer your students to the *Punctuation*, *Spelling* and *Linking expressions* sections. Students can use these to help them with their written work.

Unit 1
Are there any rooms free?

Get ready to write

- Have you ever travelled abroad as part of a group?
- Would you consider going on a group holiday now? Why? / Why not?
- Write: a one advantage of travelling as part of a group

  ----

  b one disadvantage of travelling as part of a group

  ----

  c one difficulty for an organizer trying to book a group

  ----

go to Useful language p. 82

A Asking about accommodation

Look at an example

1 **Read this email. Who is the person writing to?**
   Tick ✓ the correct answer.

   a   a hotel ☐
   b   a hotel or hostel ☐
   c   a tourist office ☐

Delete   Reply   Reply All   Forward   Print

¹Next summer I am bringing a group of 16- to 18-year-old students to Vancouver and I am looking for suitable accommodation. At present I am uncertain of the exact number of students but it will probably be about 30. While we are there, we not only want to look at the many attractions in the city, but we would like to visit some of the beautiful places nearby, so we are looking for a reasonably priced hotel or hostel near the city centre with good transport links.

²During our stay we will require the following: twin-bedded rooms in the same hotel, breakfast and, on occasions, an evening meal. We will not require lunch. We would hope that the hotel we use would be able to offer us a special rate.

³Do you have any travel consultants who could look after groups like us? For example, are you able to arrange activities and local transportation for us? Also, it would be very helpful if you could inform me of any other special discounts, such as for cheaper air travel to and from Vancouver.

⁴I look forward to hearing from you.

2 Are these sentences true (T) or false (F)?

a The first sentence makes it clear why the person is writing. _T_

b The other sentences in Paragraph 1 give background information. ......

c Paragraph 2 makes it clear what the person wants. ......

d Paragraph 3 asks for extra information. ......

e The closing sentence of the email is very informal. ......

3 Find words or phrases in the email that mean the following:

a not sure ____uncertain____ (Paragraph 1)

b not too expensive _____ (Paragraph 1)

c need _____ (Paragraph 2)

d give us a discount _____ (Paragraph 2)

e let me know _____ (Paragraph 3)

Learning tip

If you are writing to someone you know well and are friendly with, your style will be more *informal*, which means it sounds like normal conversation. Contractions, phrasal verbs, colloquial expressions and personal comments are common.

If you are writing to an institution or someone you don't know, your style will be more formal. In *very formal* language we do not usually use contractions (Not ~~don't~~ but do not ✓) or phrasal verbs (Not ~~put up~~ but accommodate ✓). The language is more impersonal and the passive voice is common.

In professional emails the style is often neither very formal nor informal. The aim is to be simple, clear and direct, and more formal or personal language is used when necessary. This is sometimes known as *neutral* language.

Plan

4 You and your partner want to spend a few days in Venice. You are going to write an email in reply to a newspaper advertisement. Read the advertisement and the notes you made. Then think about the questions below.

Venice

Beautiful apartment for rent. Perfect location, only 6 minutes' walk from the main square. Views of the Grand Canal from the terrace. Sleeps 2/4. Ideal for couples. Can accommodate short stays as well as weekly rentals. Prices from 900 euros p.w. Email: info@perfectlocation.com

Air conditioning? (July!) Internet connection? (V. imp. – need to check emails)

4 nights? Early July OK?

Price?

a Have you met the person you are writing to?

b Is the purpose of your email to get information or make a booking?

c Will your email be
   – very formal (like an old-fashioned letter e.g. beginning *Dear Sir or Madam*)?
   – informal?
   – neutral?

5 Write the points in the box in the most logical order in the paragraph plan below.

> saying how long you want to stay
> ~~saying where you saw the advertisement~~
> asking about facilities
> saying why you're writing
>
> asking about price
> closing the email
> final comment

Paragraph 1: saying where you saw the advertisement

Paragraph 2: _____

Paragraph 3: _____

Paragraph 4: _____

Paragraph 5: _____

Focus on ...
functional and fixed expressions

ab**c**def

1 Match 1–7 with a–g to make sentences.
1 I'm very interested in _d_
2 Before making a booking ......
3 (In the advertisement) you say that ......
4 I notice that ......
5 I assume ......
6 I need to know ......
7 Could you give me some idea ......

a a bit about the facilities.
b the apartment is beautifully designed.
c of the price?
d ~~coming next July with my partner.~~
e it is possible to make a booking for less than a week.
f that would be acceptable.
g I have a number of questions I would like to ask.

2 Complete these opening and closing sentences.
Opening sentence: *I saw your advertisement* (say where)

_____

Closing: *I look forward to receiving* (say what)

_____

3 Which phrase will you use to sign off the email?
1 Yours faithfully ☐
2 Cheers! ☐
3 Best wishes ☐
4 Goodbye ☐

Learning tip

When we write by hand, we often indent the first line of a new paragraph.
I have a number of questions I would like to ask.
*   You say the apartment is beautifully designed;*
However, when we write an email or a business letter we usually leave a space between paragraphs instead of indenting.

Write

6 Write a draft of your email in about 200 words.

Check

Now reread your email and answer the following questions. Make any changes that are necessary to your email.

– Is it clear to the tourist office what you want?
– Have you said when you want to come?
– Have you said how long you want to stay?
– Have you included all other necessary information?
– Is your style appropriate for the tourist office?
– Have you divided your answer into paragraphs?
– Are your paragraphs in a logical order?
– Are your spelling and punctuation correct?
– Have you chosen the best vocabulary?
– Is your grammar correct?

Class bonus

– Sit in groups and exchange your work or fix your work on the wall/board.
– Read each other's emails. Which email do you like best? Can you think of any ways to improve each other's writing?

E X tra practice

You have seen this advertisement in a magazine and you are interested in staying in the place.

CALIFORNIA BED AND BREAKFAST

Redwood House B&B. Single or double. Country setting in San Francisco Bay near Mount St. Helena. Fireplace and TV in all bedrooms. Most bathrooms with Jacuzzi and shower. Breakfast served in our sunroom or in the guests' room. $200 per night plus tax. info@redwood.com

1 Plan your answer.
2 Write your email in approximately 200 words.
3 Read your answer with the list of questions in Check. Make any necessary changes.

Did you know ...?

Private house B&Bs are common throughout Britain and the US. They are cheaper than hotels and usually have a friendly atmosphere. In Britain they usually provide a cooked breakfast, including eggs and bacon, and sometimes sausages, mushrooms and tomatoes.

Can-do checklist

Tick what you can do.

	Can do	Need more practice
I can write to a hotel to get information about services.		
I can write to find out about accommodation available.		
I can divide an email into well-organized, logically ordered paragraphs.		
I can write in a suitable style for the situation.		

Unit 2
Thanks and best wishes

Get ready to write

- You want to thank these people. Would you write an email, write a letter or phone them?
  a Your boss gave you a lift home last night. You don't know him/her very well ......
  b A friend has agreed to offer a job to someone in your family. ......
  c A distant relative has sent you a present you don't want. ......

- How polite would you be in each situation? Add a tick ✓ for 'less polite/formal', two ticks ✓✓ for 'polite/formal' and three ticks ✓✓✓ for 'very polite/formal'.

go to Useful language p. 82

A Letters of thanks and of sympathy

Look at an example

1 **Tom has written a letter to Mr Korsimbi, the Managing Director of the Thai office of Littlebytes Software. The different sections of the letter have been mixed up. Decide on the correct order of the sections.**

   Section
   1 ..D..
   2 ......
   3 ......
   4 ......
   5 ......
   6 ......
   7 ......
   8 ......

2 **Where on the page will you write your address and the date?**

A Yours sincerely

B We also want to give special thanks to your staff who at all times looked after us and made us feel very welcome. Their hospitality and general support were a great comfort to us and put our troubled minds at rest. Fortunately, my father's recovery was speedy and we were able to return home after only three weeks.

C As you know my father, who works for your London office, was seriously injured in an automobile accident while on business in Thailand a few weeks ago. As a result of your kindness and generosity, he was flown by helicopter to the Bangkok Hospital in Phuket, where he received excellent treatment and care.

D 12 Castle Street

E PS Please give Mr Sanya, who drove us everywhere, our best wishes.

F My mother and I are writing to you to express our most grateful thanks for the assistance and courtesy we received on a recent and most urgent visit to your country to see my father in hospital.

G Dear Mr Korsimbi

H We hope one day to return to Thailand on a much happier and relaxed visit. In the meantime, please give our appreciation and thanks to all concerned.

Did you know ...?

There are small differences in salutations and closings in letters in different English-speaking countries. For example:

Salutations:

Dear Mr. Smith: (US)

Dear Mr Smith or *Dear Mr Smith,* (UK)

Closings:

Sincerely, (US)

Yours sincerely or *Yours sincerely,* (UK)

In business letters there is often a subject line, which tells the reader the topic.

US   **Visit to the Thai Office**

Dear Mr. Smith:

UK

Dear Mr Smith

     Visit to the Thai Office

Learning tip

Address the reader with the correct salutation (e.g. *Dear Sir or Madam*). Always think about the person you are writing to and consider their feelings. In polite letters, be positive and respectful.

You should try and write sincerely and honestly. However, write calmly in quite formal language even if your feelings are strong.

---

3 Complete this sentence.

The main purpose of the letter is to ....

....

....

4 Is the style polite and formal, or friendly and informal?

....

5 In which section does the writer

a   give general background ...... ?

b   give the first reason for writing ...... ?

c   give the second reason for writing ..... ?

6 Tick ✓ the correct answer. The purpose of the last paragraph is:

a   to finish the letter positively (by talking about the future and repeating thanks) ☐

b   to repeat what was said at the beginning ☐

7 Write one polite phrase from each paragraph.

a   to express our most grateful thanks .....

b   ....

c   ....

d   ....

Plan

8 Read this article from a local newspaper.

Bitter taste for chocolate makers

More than 100 jobs are to be lost with the closure of a well-known chocolate factory in our region. Sweetline says the announcement is part of a global attempt to cut costs.

The announcement is a very sad one for the region since the plant has been with us for over 30 years and has become a part of the community.

The company says it will be doing all it can to inform those directly affected of alternative job opportunities and training options. It will be arranging a Jobs Fair where other local employers can exhibit and advertise job opportunities in their organizations.

Councillor Mandy Williams, Leader of Littleport County Borough Council, says: "As you would expect, we regret the current situation. We feel particularly for the individuals affected and their families. We shall do all we can to help them secure their futures."

One employee, Dave Green, who has been with the company for over ten years says, "We all love working there and we feel betrayed and disappointed. Only last month Sweetline announced that local production was up, company profits were looking healthy for the year and the factory had a good future. We don't know why they're taking this action."

Mr Green describes his three teenage children as being "devastated" by the news. "They're all very sad and worried about my future."

9 You have known Dave Green quite well for a long time, although you are not close friends. You are going to write a letter to express your sympathy with his situation. Answer the questions below.

   a Think of your relationship with Dave Green and the purpose of the letter. Will your letter be
     – very polite and formal?
     – quite polite and friendly?
     – very chatty and informal?

   b Which information will you use in your letter? Highlight or underline the key phrases.

10 Tick ✓ the points you will include in each paragraph. You may tick more than one point.

Paragraph 1: Reason for writing
Expressing regret ☐
Dave's feelings ☐
Your feelings about the closure ☐
Saying where you heard the news ☐

Paragraph 2: Giving support
Expressing hopes for the future ☐
Remembering your friendship together ☐
Talking about positive points in the article ☐

Paragraph 3: Making an offer
Offering general help ☐
Offering to try and help find Dave a job ☐
Offering to look after the children ☐

Focus on ...
polite phrases

Remember: you have known Dave quite well for some time but you are not close friends. Also, it is a difficult situation.

1 Choose the best alternative for the letter and complete the sentence.
   a I'm really sorry to hear that you / ~~Sorry about you~~ are losing your job.
   b I know how much you / Of course you really

   c No way will this mean that / I hope this doesn't mean that
   d Looking on the bright side / On a positive note
   e Please let me know if / Why not

2 Which of these will you use to finish?
   a Take care of yourself. ☐
   b I wish you the very best ☐
   c Yours sincerely ☐
   d Yours faithfully ☐

Write

11 Write a draft of your letter in about 200 words. Write today's date below your address, e.g.

     13 London Street
     Oxford
     14th December 20….

Check

12 Reread your letter and check that the letter is clear and well organized, and that the style is appropriate. Make any changes that are necessary to your answer.

13 Identify the type of mistake in each of the following extracts. Use the following code: vocabulary (V), grammar (G), punctuation (P), spelling (SP), word order (WO) or verb form (VF). Then correct the mistakes.

   a I am sorry to hear that you are loseing your job. (SP) losing
   b Having promised that only the last month the factory …
   c … while you are looking for another work.
   d Please let me know if youd like me …
   e … to look the children after at any time …
   f I hope this don't mean that …

14 Now go back to your draft and check for mistakes. Correct any mistakes you find.

Learning tip

Try and get into the habit of reviewing your work in this order.
1 Content. *Is everything included that needs to be included? Is it all relevant?*
2 Organization. *Is the text structured and divided up clearly? Does it flow logically?*
3 Style. *Is the style appropriate? Think of your relationship with the reader and the reason you are writing.*
4 Language. *Is it accurate? Is there a good range and variety? Are the tenses consistent?*
Your work is not finished until you have edited your draft and tried to improve it.

B A letter of congratulation

1 🎧**2** **You are the manager of Kingsway Travel. Magda, an ex-employee, has just graduated with an MBA (Master of Business Administration). Read the notes you made when she worked at Kingsway and listen to her message. Make notes of points to include in a letter of congratulation. Organize them under these headings:**

A Reason for writing
B Recalling the experience of working with her
C Wishing her well for the future

> APPRAISAL NOTES
>
> Magda is very intelligent and has a good business brain. She is clearly ambitious and in time will want to move on to a bigger, more demanding post elsewhere. She works extremely hard, is a good team-player and shows some leadership qualities. She always aims to give a first-class service to the customer and is polite and friendly.

2 **Write your letter of congratulation in about 200 words. Do not write an address or date. Begin your letter *On behalf of everyone here at Kingsway Travel Agency, I ...***

3 **Look at the *Audioscript* on page 90. <u>Underline</u> the most important information. Is there anything missing from your letter? Edit your answer.**

Focus on ...
word choice

Match these phrases with similar phrases from the Appraisal Notes and the answerphone message.
a You have <u>a quick mind for business</u> *a good business brain*
b You are <u>very bright</u> ....
c Your <u>ability to work with and inspire others</u>
   ....
d Your <u>strong work ethic</u> ....
e Your commitment to <u>quality customer service</u>
   ....

Class bonus

You are going to write a letter of thanks or congratulation for a situation in your school/college. Examples:
– The Principal has promised to move your class into a bigger and better room.
– A teacher is getting married.
Work in groups to brainstorm ideas and prepare a paragraph plan. Tell other groups your ideas and compare. Each group then writes a letter. Show each other the letters and decide which one to send.

Can-do checklist

Tick what you can do.

	Can do	Need more practice
I can write a polite letter of sympathy.		
I can write a polite but friendly letter of congratulation.		
I can write in a polite and formal style when necessary.		
I can write in a polite and friendly style when necessary.		
I can use a good range of appropriate vocabulary when writing.		

Unit 3
Lost!!!

Get ready to write

○ Why do people put:

a notices on noticeboards and in shop windows?

----

b small ads (small advertisements) in newspapers, magazines and on websites?

○ Tick the things people regularly use notices and small ads for in your country:
to sell a car ☐ to find a partner ☐ to offer language teaching ☐ to sell a house ☐
to find somewhere to live ☐ to find a job ☐

○ What makes a good small ad? Write one answer.

----

go to Useful language p. 83

A Small ads

Look at examples

1 Read these small ads. In which is the advertiser:

a looking for a companion? __4__
b offering accommodation? ......
c looking for help? ......
d trying to sell something? ......

2 Look carefully at the context. What do you think these abbreviations mean?

a km __kilometres__   d pw ....
b vgc ....   e inc. ....
c mins .... f no. ....

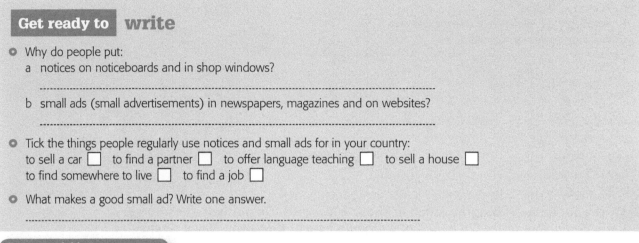

1

B&B. Beautiful location!!!.
2km Font de Gaume Caves.
South Limoges airport 25 mins.
€65 or €350 pw.
(0)555 43 30 40

2

Rover 215 SEi (1995) 150,000km.
Several new parts (inc. clutch)
Silver paintwork, leather/walnut
interior. vgc £400 for quick sale.
timely@yahoo.com

3

Volunteers needed

We are looking for <u>women aged
18–45 years</u> who may be interested
in finding out more about how
exercise affects the way our body
uses and breaks down the food
that we eat. By taking part in the
study, you will receive a detailed
health screening. If you would like
any further information, please
contact Kelly on 07980 - 65894.

4

**WARM, fun-loving
male (early 40s)** seeks
friendship and possible
long-term relationship with
independent female. Loves
opera, Mexican food and
lazing about. No smokers
please. Box no. 09/08

3 All of the ads use bold lettering to give information special attention. Which ad also uses:

a highlighting? _2_
c exclamation marks? _____
b capital letters? _____
d underlining? _____

4 In what way is ad 3 different from the other ads? What are the advantages/disadvantages of this type of ad?

----

5 All the ads are structured in a similar way. Put these in the correct order:

contact details ☐
supporting information ☐
the main point (what is being offered/looked for) [1]

Plan

6 Read the three advertisements below and complete these sentences:

Advertiser A needs ------------------------------
Advertiser B would like to improve ------------------------------
Advertiser C has lost ------------------------------

File Edit View Favorites Tools Help
Address [   ] Go Links »

A

I am a former lecturer from the University of Sydney and for the four weeks of July I am returning to Sydney with my new wife. I want to rent a flat, preferably in or near Darlington. I'd be really pleased if you were able to email me with offers at hhiggins@div.cam.edu.

B

I am a postgraduate student from Beijing. I want to speak English better. I would like to offer a language exchange with anyone who speaks Chinese. Why not give me a ring? My phone number is 06784-63109.

C

Unfortunately, we have lost our family cat, which is male and has long ginger hair. The poor thing disappeared on 4th July and we haven't seen him since. He is very timid and might run away if you see him. Naturally he is greatly missed at home so we are offering a reward of fifty dollars. If you see him – let's hope you do! – give me a ring on my mobile. My phone number is 0478-666-111.

Learning tip

– Keep your ads short and clear. Use short phrases and abbreviations (where possible).
– Choose your first word carefully. Readers will use it to find what they want.
– Structure your ad logically with the contact information last.
– For a noticeboard, highlight the most important words to make them stand out (e.g. bold/capital letters, colours, underlining, exclamation marks) but don't overdo it!

7 You are going to rewrite advertisements A–C for a university noticeboard. Tick ✓ the changes you will need to make.

add in extra information ☐
remove unnecessary words ☐
use abbreviations ☐
make the sentences longer ☐
combine information ☐
make the ad more eye-catching ☐

8 Look at advertisement A again.

a Cross out any words you could leave out. Example: I am a former lecturer…

b Which words can you abbreviate? Write some examples here. Example: weeks → wks.

----

9 Look at advertisement B again. Which information will you put:

first? _what the person wants_ ------------------------------
second? ------------------------------
third? ------------------------------

10 Look at advertisement C again. How could you change the style and keep the reader's attention? Example: *LOST!!!! Family cat.*

Did you know …?

Newspaper and magazine advertisements are often short because people have to pay for every word or line. They therefore concentrate on words which give the essential information only.

Write

11 Make a draft of your small ads here.

Check

Read your small ads and answer the following questions. Make any changes that are necessary to your answer.

- Are they concise?
- Is the purpose of each of your ads clear?
- Are the ads organized logically?
- Is the information clear?
- Have you abbreviated words where possible without making the ad confusing?
- Will the ads attract the reader's attention?
- Have I spelt verbs ending in *–ing* correctly?

Focus on ...
-ing forms and past participles

-ing forms and past participles (*-ed* forms) are commonly used in small ads.

Examples:

-ing forms:
A young man ~~who is~~ **walking** round Tibet …
I like scuba **diving** and jog**ging**.
An **exciting** time guaranteed.
I am **travelling** (Br. E) / **traveling** (Am. E) around India.

Past participles
A young man ~~who was~~ last **spotted** walking round Tibet …
(passive construction)

Complete these sentences with the correct participle form of the verb.

a Travel companion (want) _____wanted_____ for holiday in Mexico.
b I am in my thirties and (look) _____ for someone to share the (drive) _____ .
c Co-driver (seek) _____ for the journey.
d When she's not on holiday she's always on the move (do) _____ things.
e She likes (lie) _____ on the beach (watch) _____ the sun go down.
f Good (speak) _____ Spanish not necessary.
g Some desert (trek) _____ a possibility.
h Further details will be (put) _____ on the Internet.

E X tra practice 1

1 🎧 **3** Karen has decided to have a vacation in Baja California. Listen to this conversation between Karen and her friend Jessica, and <u>underline</u> the correct alternative.

The person she is looking for:

a should be a *man / woman* in *his / her teens / early twenties / mid-twenties / mid-thirties*.
b should be *serious and hardworking / relaxed and easy-going*.
c *has to / doesn't have to* be able to speak Spanish.
d *should / doesn't have to* be able to share the driving.
e *should / doesn't have to* enjoy looking at the sights.

2 Complete the sentence.
Karen enjoys such things as ....

3 You are going to write Karen's small ad for her, telling anyone who's interested to phone (619) 299-7683. Read this draft. How would you shorten it?
TRAVEL COMPANION WANTED. A woman, whose name is Karen and is in her mid-twenties (likes swimming, cycling, lying around on the beach – speaks Spanish because she used to live in Argentina, is looking for a female companion to enjoy the sights with. Contact Karen on (619) 299-7683.

4 🎧 **3** Listen again and decide if there is any other information you need to include.

5 Now write a draft of the advertisement on a separate piece of paper.

E X tra practice 2

Write a small ad for the following situation.

You have found a set of car keys (with a metal badge and a logo on it) for a luxury car in the Castle Hill area of the city. They were probably dropped by someone walking their dog. If anyone thinks they belong to them, they should come to the reception at Shelley's Bookshop and identify them.

Class bonus

Start a small ad section on your classroom noticeboard. Decide on categories: e.g. *For Sale*, *For Rent*, *Wanted*, *Free*, *Exchange*. Either with another student or individually, write a small ad for the board. Maintain the board on a regular basis.

Can-do checklist

Tick what you can do.

	Can do	Need more practice
I can write a short, clear small ad for a noticeboard.		
I can write a small ad for a newspaper/magazine etc.		
I can structure a small ad logically.		
I can use abbreviations in notices.		
I can use participles in notices.		

Fill in this form, please

Get ready to write

- Tick ✓ the application forms you have filled in recently
  - to join a club ☐   for a visa ☐
  - to open a bank account ☐   for a job ☐
  - Others: _____

- Which did you fill in online? _____

- Write these details for yourself:
  - Title [Mr/Mrs/Miss/Ms]: _____
  - First name: _____
  - Middle initial(s): _____
  - Surname: _____
  - Date of birth: _____

go to Useful language p. 83

A Complex forms

Look at examples

1 Which of the forms A–D is an application form

a for a vehicle licence? _3_

b for a supermarket 'loyalty' card? _____

c to open a bank account? _____

d for a language course? _____

1

Bank account application

name	Megan J Simmons
DOB	18/12/1990
sex	Female
email address	megan@onerly.com
marital status	Single
type of account applied for	● Single ○ Joint

2

English in York   Registration Form Courses for Adults

Personal information

Family name: *Morioka*	First names: *Natsu*
Title: *Miss*	Male ☐ Female ☑

First language: *Japanese*   Nationality: *Japanese*   Occupation: *Journalist*

Correspondence address: *12-2, Roppongi, Meguro-ku*

City: *Tokyo*   Postcode: *100-000 4*   Country: *Japan*

Accommodation options Please tick here if you have arranged your own accommodation ☐

☐ Standard – single room with a shared bathroom, breakfast and evening meals
☑ Executive – single room with a private bathroom, breakfast and evening meals

Do you have any special dietary or other requirements? *None*
Do you have a medical condition or any allergies? *None*
Do you smoke? Yes ☐ No ☑

Payment details *Please tick when you wish to pay your fees:*

☑ I wish to pay the total fees now

Or I wish to pay a deposit of £150 (UK) or €250 and the registration fee (both items are non-refundable) now and the balance or fees or first instalment six weeks before my course begins.

Note: If you are paying a deposit and registration fee only, please indicate how you wish to pay your balance of fees by ticking one of the boxes below:
Credit card ☑   Bank transfer ☐   Cheque (UK only) ☐

Credit/Debit card

Please charge the: Total fees ☑ OR Deposit & registration fee ☐ to my:
Visa / Mastercard / Maestro / American Express *(Delete as applicable)*

Card number (Visa / Mastercard / Maestro)
7 7 8 4 1 9 9 7 2 0 6 3 7 9 6 2

Expiry Date: 0 7 0 9   Issue number: ☐☐ *(Maestro only)*

Card holder name: *Natsu Morioka*   Card holder signature: *Natsu Morioka*

3

Vehicle Details

1. Registration mark
Please write clearly in the boxes
(An incorrect or unclear entry could result in further enquiries or an incorrect licence disk being issued).

   W 8 3 9 P L L

2. Taxation class of licence required
(such as Private/Light Goods [PLG], Petrol Car etc   *PETROL CAR*

3. Make and model e.g (Rover 414, Vauxhall Corsa, Ford Mondeo) *Nissan Micra*

4. Mileage (to the last complete mile)   1 0 2 1 1 0

Licence Details

5. State whether the licence is to run for 6 or 12 months _6_ months

6. State clearly in the boxes, the month and year you want the licence to start   0 1 0 5 0 8

4

Complete this form to receive your Shopper points

All about you
Title: Mr ☒   Mrs ☐   Miss ☐   Ms ☐

First name(s): Y U S U F   Surname: B U R A K G A Z I

House no: 6 6   Street, Town/City: M A N O R   C O U R T
M I T C H A M   Postcode: C B 7 1 P P

Contact details
Preferred contact number: (home, work, mobile)
0 1 3 5 6   4 4 7 6 9 9

Household details
How many people are there in your household? (including yourself) 3
Please enter the ages of the people in your household, other than yourself
Age 2 4   Age 2 3   Age 1   Age 1   Age 1

Dietary needs
Please tick if you have any of the following dietary requirements.
Diabetic ☐   Vegetarian ☐   Teetotal ☐   Kosher ☐   Halal ☑

Your signature   Date
Yusuf Burakgazi   0 7 0 9 2 0 0 8

2 Which form was completed online?

----

3 Look at form 1 again.

a Is Megan married?

----

b What kind of account does she want?

----

4 Look at form 2 again.

a Where does Natsu come from?

----

b What kind of accommodation does she want?

----

c How will she pay her fees?

----

5 Look at form 3 again.

a How many miles has the car done?

----

b What month will the licence start from?

----

6 Look at form 4 again.

a How old are the people living in his house?

----

b What kind of diet does Yusuf follow?

----

7 Find an example of where

a the form has been completed in capital letters.
b letters have been written without joining them together.

Learning tip

When filling in a form:
- write neatly, using block capitals where possible
- check your spelling. You don't want to be misunderstood
- make sure you have put the details in the correct space
- use the symbols required (e.g. ticks ✓ and crosses ✗)
- learn to write out numbers correctly.

Did you know …?

Women often prefer to use *Ms* instead of *Miss* or *Mrs* because it does not draw attention to their marital status.

Focus on …
writing numbers in words

How do you write these numbers in words?

a	3 _three_		3rd _third_	
b	13th _____		13 _____	
c	30th _____		31st _____	
d	4th _____		14th _____	
e	1st _____		12th _____	
f	9th _____		99 _____	
g	25 _____		25th _____	
h	8th _____		88 _____	
i	2nd _____		22nd _____	

Look at this example:

BANK us

Date _____

Pay Twelve Dollars and 25 Cents only

$ 12.25

Mr.A.N.OTH

BANK PLC

Cheque no 00378   Sort Code 61 1745   Account no 0999676

Write these figures as you would write them on a cheque.

j $450 _____

k £1,115.13 _____

l €275 _____

Plan

8 You want to send some money abroad by MoneyGram®. Match the headings in A with their definitions in B.

A

a Destination
b Receiver
c Transaction
d Signature
e Sender

B

1 The amount of money you are sending
2 Your name as you usually write it
3 The place it is going to
4 Your personal details
5 The person you are sending it to

9 Answer these questions.

a Will you write the letters individually or joined together?
b Will you use only capital letters?

Send Form   PLEASE COMPLETE IN BLOCK CAPITALS   **MoneyGram.**
International Money Transfer

S/001c Rev 02/06

DESTINATION

Country
City
Is there a suitable receive agent at the above destination? If not please ask staff to confirm

AGENT USE ONLY

Office Name/Stamp
(either/or)

SENDER

Title (please tick)   Mr.   Mrs.   Ms.   Miss.   Other (please state)
First Name
Middle Name
Surname
Date of Birth (optional)   D D M M Y Y Y Y
Address
Town/City
Postcode
Country
Contact Tel No.
Please include area code

Date   D D M M Y Y Y Y
MoneyGram Operator ID Number   For voice transactions only
Amount Sent
Consumer Fee
Total to be Collected

For transactions requiring ID:-
Sender's ID
Type of ID and number

RECEIVER

Title (please tick)   Mr.   Mrs.   Ms.   Miss.   Other (please state)
First Name
Middle Name
Surname

Issuing Jurisdiction State/Country

For transactions requiring additional information:-
Senders Date of Birth   D D M M Y Y Y Y
Sender's occupation

TRANSACTION

Amount to be sent
In words and figures

In figures
Test Question
Answer
Message
Max 10 words

Receive Information   Only complete this once the transaction has been sent
Receive currency
Exchange rate
Received amount
OR
US Currency   USD
Received Amount
Receive Country pays out in USD?   Y   N
Exchange rate may apply   (Please tick)

SIGNATURE

The undersigned waives any right he or she may have to receive a written report of this transaction pursuant to Cross-Border Credit Transfer Regulations 1999. This transaction is subject to the terms and conditions on the reverse of this form. Please note, if this transaction is sent on behalf of a 3rd party you must fill in the reverse of this form. Take care when sending money to someone that you do not know and when asked to pass information about the transactions to third parties.

Sender's signature _____   Date   D D M M Y Y Y Y

Reference No.

MoneyGram may use the information provided on this form for the purpose of sending you further information about the services offered by MoneyGram. If you do not wish to receive such information, please tick this box. ☐

Distribution: Top Copy - Agent   Bottom Copy - Customer   Code P5032/2

This is a Multipart Set. Please use a Ball Point Pen
© TM 2006 MoneyGram Payment Systems Inc. The MoneyGram logo is a service mark of MoneyGram Payment Systems Inc.
25487
ACCESS PLUS

Write

10 Complete the sender details with information about yourself.

11 🔘④ You have asked a friend to help you complete the MoneyGram® form. Listen to your friend's advice and complete the rest of the form with the details you hear.

12 Sign and date the form.

Check

Read your form through and check that:

– you have included all the information that is required under each heading
– all the letters are capitals
– your spelling is correct
– your handwriting is clear and easy to read

Check your answer against the *Audioscript* on page 90 and make any necessary changes.

E X tra practice

1 You are going on a skiing holiday with at least one member of your family. Decide who you are going with, where you are going and the dates you will be away. Complete the application form for your travel insurance.

1. Name and Address of first named person (Principal Insured)

Title (Mr/Mrs/Ms/Miss) Initials Surname Date of Birth Age

House Nº Address Line 1 Address Line 2

Address Line 3 Postcode Telephone

Mobile Email Address

3. Cover Type — Complete the box for either Single Trip Cover or Annual

Single Trip Cover (max 90 day trip)

Country of Destination

Departure Date Return Date No. of Days*

*Inclusive of day of departure from your home/business and day of return to your home/business.

Travel Insurance Type (please mark appropriate boxes with an **X**)

☐ Individual   ☐ Lone Parent

☐ Family   ☐ Couple

☐ Ski/Winter Sport

Area ☐ UK   ☐ Europe

☐ Worldwide   ☐ Worldwide
(excl USA, Canada   (incl USA, Canada
and the Caribbean)   and the Caribbean)

2 Read the form through and check that it is clear and accurate.

Class bonus

1 Before you come to class, go on the Internet and download one of these application forms:
   - a temporary resident's permit for an English-speaking country, e.g. Canada or New Zealand
   - an application form for a job in a UK hotel. Use your search engine to help you (e.g. enter: *hotel job application form uk*)
   - an application form for a place in a US university.

2 Complete the form for yourself.
3 Mix up and distribute all the application forms.
4 Read out some details on the application form you receive to give clues about the person, but don't give obvious information (e.g. the person's name).
5 Ask other students to guess who it is.

Can-do checklist

Tick what you can do.

	Can do	Need more practice
I can understand the headings on an application form.		
I can complete a form clearly and accurately.		
I can use the correct spelling on a form.		
I can use the requested style (e.g. capital letters).		
I can write figures in words.		

Unit 5
The most amazing place!

go to Useful language p. 83

Get ready to write

- When you travel, do you like to write about the place you are in?
  Tick ✓ which of these you do:
  keep a diary ☐
  write a travel blog ☐
  describe the place in an email ☐, in a letter ☐, on a postcard ☐

- Give one reason you write about places you visit:
  ....

A Email describing a place

Look at an example

1 Compare these two email opening paragraphs. Which one (A or B) is written to

friends? ......
grandparents? ......

2 Underline the correct alternative.

a The email to the grandparents uses *more* / *less* colloquial language.

b The email to friends sounds *more* / *less* relaxed and informal.

c The email to the grandparents is *more* / *less* personal.

3 Write an example from email B of colloquial language commonly used by young people.

----

4 The purpose of the opening paragraph is to:

a say why you like or don't like the place ☐

b give the context by saying where you are ☐

5 Underline the most likely opening for:

a the email to friends: *Hello everybody.* / *Hi all*

b the email to grandparents: *Dear Grandmother and Grandfather* / *Hello Grandma and Grandpa* / *Hi folks*

A

> New Reply Reply all Forward ✗ Delete Junk   Move to

I'm still in India. I'm in a place in the east of India called Bodh Gaya, about 100 km from Patna. It's a very interesting place. It's where people believe that the Buddha found enlightenment under the Bodhi Tree.

B

> New Reply Reply all Forward ✗ Delete Junk   Move to

I'm writing this from an internet café in one very cool place called Bodh Gaya – that's about 100k or so from Patna in east India for you guys who don't know too much about geography. If you're not a Buddhist, you've probably never heard of it, but if you meditate in Buddhist retreats back home like I do, you'll know it's where people believe Buddha found enlightenment under the Bodhi Tree.

6 **Read the rest of the email to friends, on the right. Write 1, 2, 3 or 4 in the boxes to describe the function of each paragraph.**

talks about where the person is going next ☐
gives general impressions ☐
gives the key features of the place ☐ 1
talks about disadvantages ☐

7 **Write an example of**

a repeating a word for emphasis

----

b adding an auxiliary verb for emphasis

----

c *so* + adjective to express enthusiasm

----

d another adverb + adjective combination

The town is really, really tiny. Ordinary tourists do everything in less than half a day. The temples are all very close together and you can see the Tree from almost anywhere in the town. But most people here are pilgrims from all over the world and they come to meditate.

This place is so peaceful. You feel so relaxed just being here. This morning I looked out from my hotel roof at sunrise – it was amazingly beautiful – and watched the people in the fields and the women making bricks for their fire.

The only frustrating thing is that we do get a lot of powercuts, so I'll send this now before I lose everything!

Tomorrow I'm setting off for Varanasi. Wish me luck!

Plan

8 **You have just walked the four-day Milford Track in New Zealand and want to write an email to tell your friend, Areefa, about it. Read the information below and complete the sentences.**

a My email will be personal and informal because

----

b I want to create a vivid picture for Areefa so I will use

----

c In my first paragraph I will tell Areefa

----

d In my main paragraph(s) I will describe

----

e In my final paragraph I will tell Areefa

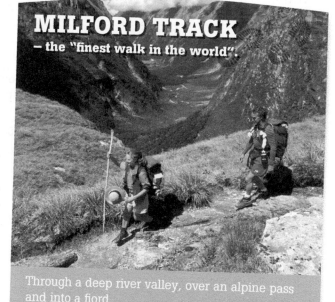

MILFORD TRACK
– the "finest walk in the world".

Through a deep river valley, over an alpine pass and into a fiord.
Length: 53.5 km

Day one – 3.5 km Glade Wharf to Clinton Hut Fine.

Day two – Clinton Hut to Mintaro Hut 16.5 km

Day three – Mintaro Hut to Dumpling Hut 14 km

Day four – Dumpling Hut to Sandfly Point 18 km

Along the flat. Took nearly 15 hrs. Weather calm.

Exhausting (over 5 hrs walking!) Incredible views of valley – river looked a turquoise colour.

(6hrs) The views at the top of Mackinnon Pass!! Wow! One of wettest places on earth but it was SUNNY!!!

(6 hrs) cold and wet! – suddenly there were waterfalls in the valley – mist and cloud. Mysterious – my photographs don't really convey the atmosphere.

Learning tip

When writing an email or travel blog and describing a place
- structure your text into paragraphs that each have a separate focus
- give interesting details that will help bring the place to life, but don't give so many details that it gets boring
- convey your feelings to the reader and give your general impressions
- use a range of adjectives and modifying adverb + adjective combinations (*fairly/really attractive, quite/rather fashionable, utterly/absolutely charming, extremely/remarkably relaxing*).

Focus on ...
capital letters and punctuation

Write these extracts with appropriate capital letters and punctuation. Use *Appendix 2* to help you.

1 how are you after i left you in cape town i decided to get a cheap flight to new zealand because i wanted to walk along the milford track have you heard about it

----

----

2 luckily we were blessed with sunny weather which is amazing since mackinnon pass is one of the wettest places on earth unfortunately on the last day the weather broke and it poured down and was quite cold

----

----

9 **Write 1, 2, 3, 4, 5 to show the logical order of these sentences to make a paragraph. There may be more than one possible answer.**

My regret was that you weren't there with me. ☐
Anyway, from here I'm planning to travel a bit more around South Island. ☐
I'll just have to keep everything in my memory. ☐
You would have loved the whole trek. ☐
Although I took lots of pictures I know that none of the pictures will do the place justice. ☐1

Did you know ...?

Annually, over 250,000 students in the UK from all social classes take gap years in their education.
Most gap years involve travel for at least a part of the time, with Australia being the most popular destination.
Young people fund their year through paid work, savings, sponsorship and parental help. There are a large number of organizations to support them.

Write

10 **Write a draft of your email. Try to write between 200 and 250 words. Use the ideas in the *Learning tip* to help you.**

Check

Read your email. Underline the correct alternative.

- My email *will / will not* interest the reader.
- The first paragraph *does / does not* say what I'm doing in the place.
- I *have / have not* said what each day of the walk was like.
- I *have / have not* written a concluding paragraph.
- The purpose of each paragraph *is / is not* clear.
- I *have used some / haven't used any* adverb + adjective combinations.
- My use of capital letters and punctuation *is / isn't* accurate.

Make any changes that are necessary to your answer.

Learning tip

It is a good idea to have a break between writing the email and checking it.
When checking the draft of an email:
- have the line you are checking at the bottom of the screen. This will give your eyes an easy amount to read.
- read the email aloud. This will slow you down and help you concentrate.

B Writing a travel blog

1 Have you ever been here? Look at the photograph and write one phrase, to include an adjective, which you think describes it.

Rio de Janeiro from Sugar Loaf Mountain

2 🔊 **5** Kaya is in Rio on holiday. Listen to her internet telephone call to her friend Melinda and make notes under these headings.

a The view from Sugar Loaf Mountain

----

b The hotel

----

c The beaches

----

d Comparing Rio with other cities

----

e The people

----

3 Write Kaya's travel blog for today on a separate piece of paper. Each sentence has been started for you.

Paragraph 1
Rio is one of the most *beautiful cities in the world.*
To really appreciate …
You'll see how …

Paragraph 2
Our hotel in Rio is …
It is just round …
Of course we do the …

Paragraph 3
The beaches are …
Just today we went …
People here play …
It's the most …

Paragraph 4
For me, Rio is much the same …
The streets …
The only difference …

Paragraph 5
One of the things I like most …
Brazil is …
People really are …

4 Check your travel blog. Use the checklist on page 28 to help.

Class bonus

– Choose a place other students in the class don't know, e.g. the place where you go on holiday. Write a paragraph to describe one or two key features. Make your description as vivid as possible.
– Read a paragraph written by another student and ask questions to find out more information.
– Get back your paragraph and make notes of extra information you think would be interesting.
– Write an email to a penfriend describing the place.

Can-do checklist

Tick what you can do.

	Can do	Need more practice
I can write an email describing a place.		
I can write a travel blog.		
I can use adjective phrases to make a description vivid.		
I can use capital letters and punctuation correctly.		

Unit 6
I thought it was great!

go to Useful language pp. 83–4

Get ready to write

- Read these two reviews quickly. Which one is about: a a restaurant? ......   b a computer game? ......

http://www.reviewsonline.com

1

I've played over 80 hours and thoroughly enjoyed it so far. For the fun it provides and the sheer beauty I would give it 5 stars, but perhaps only 3 for the way the enemy levels are structured. I can see that after a time it might get a bit boring.

2

★★★★ **Overall, very good!**
Good points
Their Italian beef sandwiches are OUTSTANDING!!! And I love the fact it's open all night.
Bad points
They only sell their GREAT BBQ Baby Back Ribs between 4pm and midnight.
General comments
If you love Chicago Food you need to check it out. It can get crowded, particularly in the evenings. So get there early!

Which phrases help you decide? <u>Underline</u> the *positive* phrases in each review.

- Does reading a review ever influence your decision to buy something or go somewhere?

A Review

Look at an example

1 Read this review of a DVD and answer the questions.

a Where might you find a review like this?

----

b Do you think it is written by a professional reviewer?

Full of life and fantastic music, this movie is a resounding success. Not just a well-directed and well-edited biopic of the American country singer, Johnny Cash, it also tells the story of his early love and friendship with June Carter, the woman he later married.

What definitely lifts the story above the average biopic are wonderful performances from the two main characters. Everybody has praised Reese Witherspoon as June Carter. She's the best thing in the movie – comical and moving – and definitely deserved the Oscar, but I thought Joaquin Phoenix was pretty good too and captured Cash's darker moods really well. Amazingly, Witherspoon and Phoenix actually sang the tracks themselves and they're surprisingly effective, though the real Cash had a singing voice that was slightly rougher.

My only complaint is that as a biopic the movie is not comprehensive enough. We don't get to know much about Cash's life before 1955 and the film ends with his marriage to June in 1968. Even more disappointing is that we don't really find out what happens to his first wife and two children once she leaves him.

All the same, watch the movie and you will understand what it means to be two talented, highly individual people, living in a world that expects you to behave like everyone else.

2 Tick ✓ the correct alternatives.

a The first sentence
  catches the reader's attention. ☐
  gives some detailed information. ☐
b The second sentence
  talks about the acting. ☐
  makes it clear what the film is about. ☐
c In the first two paragraphs the reviewer
  gives the main reasons for enjoying the film. ☐
  compares it with another film. ☐
d In the third paragraph the reviewer
  expresses some reservations about the film. ☐
  gives the good and the bad points. ☐
e In the last paragraph the reviewer
  repeats what was said at the beginning. ☐
  gives a personal recommendation. ☐

3 Circle the adverb that *can't* be used with the word in bold.

a a *great / wide / resounding* **success**
b *utterly / well- / carefully* **edited**
c *totally / fairly / definitely* **deserved** the Oscar
d was *completely / pretty / quite* **good** too
e *remarkably / surprisingly / practically* **effective**

4 Underline the correct linking expression.

a Reese Witherspoon was good *but / however* Joaquin Phoenix was very good too.
b Phoenix sang pretty well, even *so / though* the real Cash had a hoarser voice.
c Unfortunately, the film ends in 1968. *Even more / Moreover*, disappointing is that we don't find out what happens to his first wife. *What's more, / All the same,* watch the movie with an open mind and you will enjoy it.

Did you know ...?

– When we talk about movies in general we often use these terms:
  blockbuster: a large, very successful movie;
  world cinema / foreign films: used in English-speaking countries for films from non-English-speaking countries;
  art house movies: usually foreign-language films or films made by small companies.
– We also talk about different genres (categories) of movies like *biopic* (the life story of a particular person), *romantic comedy* (or *rom com*), *epic drama* (a long movie with a lot of action about an historical subject), *science fiction* (or *sci-fi*). We also talk about an *adaptation* from a famous novel, like *Sense and Sensibility*, or a *remake* of a classic movie, like *King Kong*.

Plan

5 An online bookstore has asked its customers to send in a review of this book. Read this summary and the notes you made. Answer questions a and b below.

a What is the aim of your review?

  ----

b Tick ✓ which style you will use:
  formal ☐
  fairly informal ☐
  neutral ☐

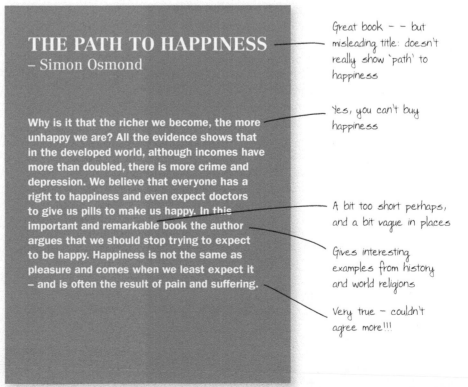

THE PATH TO HAPPINESS
– Simon Osmond

Why is it that the richer we become, the more unhappy we are? All the evidence shows that in the developed world, although incomes have more than doubled, there is more crime and depression. We believe that everyone has a right to happiness and even expect doctors to give us pills to make us happy. In this important and remarkable book the author argues that we should stop trying to expect to be happy. Happiness is not the same as pleasure and comes when we least expect it – and is often the result of pain and suffering.

Great book – – but misleading title: doesn't really show 'path' to happiness

Yes, you can't buy happiness

A bit too short perhaps, and a bit vague in places

Gives interesting examples from history and world religions

Very true – couldn't agree more!!!

6 This is an example of a paragraph plan for the review. What would you include in paragraphs 2–4? Make notes.

Paragraph 1: Introduction, making it clear whether you like it or not
Read book without stopping. Deeply inspiring. Wisdom on every page. Bits I'll remember forever.

Paragraph 2: Giving some idea of what it's about

Paragraph 3: Any reservations

Paragraph 4: Giving a recommendation

Focus on ...
linking expressions

Some words which link parts of a sentence together are *conjunctions*. (*I like him,* **even though** *he can be annoying at times.*) Some words which link ideas across sentences are either *adverbs* (*I don't want to go.* **Besides***, it's too late.*) or connecting expressions like *in addition*.

	Conjunctions	Adverbs and other connecting expressions
Addition	*as well as*	*besides, in addition, in fact*
Contrast	*although, even though*	*however, nevertheless, even so, on the other hand*
Connection	*similarly*	
Alternatives	*or*	*in other words*

Other phrases
Giving reasons: *because of this*
Giving examples: *for instance, such as*
Being more exact: *that is to say*

Underline the correct linking expression. Check any expressions you don't understand in a dictionary.
a   I found this book deeply inspiring *even so* / *as well as* very thought-provoking.
b   We know that money can't buy us happiness. *For instance* / *However*, Osmond gives us many other bits of wisdom, *because of this* / *such as* that we should stop looking for happiness.
c   Happiness is not the same as pleasure. *Besides* / *Similarly*, each of us experiences happiness differently.
d   He tells us a lot about the major religions. *In other words* / *In addition*, he refers us to some useful websites.
e   My main complaint is that the book is a bit vague in places. *That is to say* / *Nevertheless*, it's a very good read.
f   The book's fairly short. *In fact,* / *On the other hand* it's rather too short.

Write

7 Write a draft of your review in about 200 words.

Check

Think of the type of mistakes you make when you are writing. Which of these do you make most often ✓ and which do you make least often ✗?

verb tenses/forms (e.g. *he* ~~*has gone*~~ *went there yesterday*) ☐
articles (*a/the*) ☐
punctuation ☐
word order ☐
paragraphs ☐
spelling ☐
noun or verb endings (*I think → he thinks*) ☐
linking expressions ☐
register (the right style for the context) ☐

Read your draft and check what types of mistakes you have made. Then think about these questions.

– Will your review catch the reader's attention?
– Is the plot summary sufficiently brief but clear?
– Have you included negative as well as positive points?
– Have you used evaluative adjectives and adverbs?
– Have you given your personal recommendation?

Make any changes that are necessary to your draft.

Learning tip

Remember that a review is not just a summary of facts, it's also your opinion. The reader needs to know something about the content of a film, book etc. but keep your summary brief. Focus on the opinions and impressions that you think are the most important.

E X tra practice

1 You have been asked to write a review for an international magazine of a TV programme you have seen recently. Make notes under these headings:
   - What the programme is about
   - What's good about it
   - What's not so good about it
   - Whether you can recommend it. How many stars would you give it? (***** = outstanding/highly recommended; *** = average but nothing special; * = rubbish)

2 Tick any of these which describe the programme:
   great family entertainment ☐   highly watchable ☐
   a bit flat ☐   extremely popular ☐
   totally unconvincing ☐   truly original ☐
   incredibly boring ☐   absolutely hilarious ☐
   compulsive viewing ☐   really lively ☐

3 Organize your notes into a logical sequence and decide how many paragraphs you need.

4 Decide on an opening sentence that will catch the reader's attention.

5 Write your review in about 200 words.

Class bonus

Choose a film you have all seen, or watch a DVD together as a class.
Work in pairs or groups. Agree on things like:
- the main idea of the film
- the quality of the direction, photography and music
- your overall impression/opinion.
In your pairs or groups, write a review.
Fix the reviews to the wall or noticeboard, or exchange reviews with another pair/group. How is your review different from the others?

Can-do checklist

Tick what you can do.

	Can do	Need more practice
I can write an informal review for a website.		
I can write persuasively.		
I can use adverb + adjective combinations for personal opinions.		
I can use linking expressions correctly.		

A Structuring an email

1 Read the first part of this email. Sentences 1 and 5 are in the correct order. The others are jumbled. Why is the person writing? Tick ✓ the correct answer.

a To cancel a booking. ☐
b To ask for further information. ☐
c To make a booking. ☐

2 What style is the person writing in?

a neutral (neither very formal nor very informal) ☐
b personal ☐

3 Write 2–4 to show the correct order of the jumbled sentences.

4 Now read the second part of the email. Write 7–13 to show the correct order of the sentences.

5 Divide the sentences into five paragraphs. Write the numbers of the sentences you have written above.

Paragraph 1: ..1, 2..
Paragraph 2: ....
Paragraph 3: ....
Paragraph 4: ....
Paragraph 5: ....

File Edit View Insert Format Tools Message Help

I have seen on your website that you have villas to rent in the south of Portugal. ☐1

However, the villa we're interested in only has four bedrooms. ☐

First, let me say that we are coming with another family and we're looking for a place which will sleep 10 people. ☐

I am particularly interested in the one with the Reference No. P2710 and would like some more details. ☐

Could you tell me how many beds there are in each? ☐5

My next point is that we are planning to come in July, which is probably your busiest period. ☐6

In the meantime, could you tell me what availability you have? ☐

Thank you in advance. ☐

At this stage we don't know the exact dates, but I should know shortly. ☐

Are there any that I need to be worried about? ☐

However, the one thing that worries me is that it might be a bit noisy at night if there are nightclubs nearby. ☐

Lastly, I'd like to know something about the location. ☐

One of the things that attracts me to the villa is that it is close to the beach and has spectacular views. ☐

I look forward to hearing from you. ☐14

B Making a small ad

Rewrite the information below to make it suitable for a small ad. Use capital letters, exclamation marks, etc. where appropriate.

I've got a Pentium 3 laptop for sale. It has a 20 Gigabyte Hard Disk. The laptop is in very good condition. I'm throwing in a free laptop bag for good luck. The whole lot costs only £600. Please phone me on 07645-732651.

C Completing a form

Paul Roberts is a doctor. He wishes to visit a friend who lives overseas from 15th to 30th September next year. Look at the extracts from his passport and driving licence and complete this extract from a visa application form.

United Kingdom of Great Britain and Northern Ireland

Surname ROBERTS	**Passport No.** 31688543
Given names PAUL ANTHONY	
Nationality BRITISH CITIZEN	
Date of birth 11 JUL 74	
Sex M	**Place of birth** WOKING
Date of issue 1 MAR 06 UKPA	**Authority** **Date of expiry** 1 MAR 16

25

DRIVING LICENCE
UK
1. ROBERTS
2. PAUL ANTHONY
8. 96 HULL ROAD, CARDIFF BA7 9RR
9. B,BE,C1,C1E,D1,D1E,*f,k,l,p*

VISA DEPARTMENT

Please complete the application form in CAPITAL LETTERS and BLACK INK.

Title: Mr / Mrs / Miss / Ms / (Dr) Other: ....   Surname: ....

First Name: ....   Middle Name: ....

Maiden Name: ....

Date of Birth: ....   Place of Birth: ....   Nationality: ....

Passport No: .... Date of Issue: ....   Date of Expiry: ....

Passport issued by (Authority/Agency) ....

Occupation: ....

Permanent Address: ....   Postcode ....

Reason for visit: ....

Date of arrival: ....   Date of departure: ....

Date: ....   Signature of Applicant ....

D Writing a review

1 This is an advertisement for a hotel and some notes you made after your visit. Complete the review below for a hotel booking website.

Quality Rest Hotel — Not bad/q. good value for money

This modern hotel is superbly situated just minutes away from the University in the heart of Oxford and successfully combines convenience and comfort. — true, but had to park in expensive public car park (no hotel parking)

v. small for a double room, only shower

tasteful, contemporary

All rooms are decorated to an exceptionally high standard – and include colour TV and high-speed internet access. — remote control not working/hotel v. slow to replace

not free – pay by the hour

Dinner is served in our restaurant on the ground floor and buffet breakfast is between 8.00 am and 9.30 am. — nice food, good prices

no imagination (no fruit); bad coffee; just toast, cheese, yoghurt

---

We stayed at the Quality Rest Hotel in the centre of Oxford last week for two nights. It is _____ the city centre, but unfortunately there _____ car park nearby. The room was _____ and the decoration _____ . However, it was very _____ . Also, there were two minor irritations. The remote control _____ _____ .

The evening restaurant is _____ but the buffet breakfast _____ . All we had was _____ _____ . All in all, _____ , but I wouldn't recommend it _____ .

2 <u>Underline</u> the correct alternative.

a Oxford was *extremely* / <u>*absolutely*</u> freezing when we went.
b The nights were *absolutely* / *bitterly* cold.
c I thought the university was *a bit* / *remarkably* beautiful.
d The Ashmolean Museum was *particular* / *particularly* interesting.
e Some of the exhibits were absolutely *fascinated* / *fascinating* .
f My husband was *disappointed* / *disappointing* by the hotel.

E Writing formally

This is a letter of thanks, written in a neutral style. Choose the most appropriate phrase below to complete each gap.

Dear Ms Nemec

(a) ..1.. on behalf of everyone working in our charity (b) ...... for the money you (c) ...... in the recent crisis. (d) ...... start rebuilding their lives.

(e) ...... we responded immediately by (f) ...... and emergency supplies. We were able to be of direct benefit to thousands of lives.

(g) ...... for the unfortunate victims but your assistance will (h) ....

Thank you for (i) ....

(j) ......

a 1 I am writing   2 I thought I'd drop you a line
b 1 to say thanks   2 to thank you
c 1 raised in support of our relief efforts
  2 managed to get from everyone to help us out
d 1 No doubt about it – what you did will help them
  2 Your contribution will assist those in the affected areas to
e 1 Right after the crisis   2 After the tragic events
f 1 helping out with money, people
  2 providing financial assistance, personnel
g 1 It'll be ages before things are all right
  2 The process of recovery will be a very slow one
h 1 make long-term recovery possible
  2 make it OK for them in the long-run
i 1 being so nice to us at this time
  2 your generosity and support of this vital effort
j 1 Yours sincerely   2 Take care

F Writing accurately

There are a number of mistakes in this student's email. Look at the correction code and read the text. Write the code for the type of mistake in a, and then write the correct answer in b.

V: vocabulary   G: grammar   P: punctuation
SP: spelling   WO: word order   VF: verb form

Thanks for the email. Did I tell you Ive (1a ..P..
b ......I've......) started to look for accomodation
(2a ...... b ....) in vancouver? (3a ......
b ....) My job here come (4a ......
b ....) to an end next month and last
week a travel company offered me a great job in that
fantastic city. Could you some idea give to me
(5a ...... b ....) of the best places to live?
Would you recomend (6a ...... b ....) the
waterfront area or is that too expensive? Is it a long
travel (7a ...... b ....) to get from there to
the downtown area?

I look forward to hear (8a ...... b ....)
from you soon.

G Reflecting

What are the most important things you learnt in Units 1–6?

Which units/sections did you find most useful?

Which writing tasks did you find the easiest?

Which writing tasks do you still need more practice in?

Unit 7
Keep it brief

Write answers to the following questions.
- Why does a journalist make notes:
  a before they interview someone?

  ----

  b during the interview?

- When might an employee leave a note for a manager?

  ----

go to Useful language p. 84

A Notes and messages

Look at examples

1 Match the short notes and messages A–E with the people 1–5.

1 Student ..B..   2 Trainer .....   3 Restaurant critic .....   4 Interviewer .....   5 Travel agent .....

A

The McKenzies — 2 wks. Poland
and Hung. Pref. 3* hotels if
avail. but 2* OK if nec. Train
— NO COACHES!!!

B

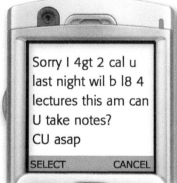

Sorry I 4gt 2 cal u
last night wil b l8 4
lectures this am can
U take notes?
CU asap

SELECT   CANCEL

C

In gen. v. trad. steak and roast
pots. ✓✓✓ Vgtarian ok but
v. little choice. Rsnble price.

D

SESSION 1
Intro. to home computing

Personal qs. – yr. experiences????
If nec. talk about basic equip. r'q'rd (eg modem) +
uses (email/internet etc.)
c.f. software applctns.

E

Cand. No. 5. good prof.
b/grnd – <u>100% IT</u>.
Lively & enthus. NB
– prefers p.t. if poss.

2 Many standard abbreviations come from Latin. Match the abbreviations in the box with their definitions below.

a.m.	etc.	~~e.g.~~	c.f.	NB

a for example ...*e.g.*...   d compare ....
b take note ....   e and so on ....
c in the morning ....

3 Look again at messages A–E on the opposite page. Find an abbreviation that means:

a very .....x.....   d information technology ....
b part time ....   e as soon as possible ....
c weeks ....

4 When people send text messages, numbers and letters sometimes represent the sound of words, e.g. **4gt** means *forgot*. Look at message B. What do these mean?

a 2 cal u ....
b CU ....
c l8 ....

5 Look again at the notes and messages in Exercise 1 and expand the notes into full sentences. Do not use abbreviations. Use more than one sentence if necessary.

A The McKenzies would like to spend _two weeks in Poland and_
Hungary.
....

B Sorry, I ....
....
....

C In general, the food was..
....
....
....

D In the introduction to home computing the trainer will ....
....
....

E Candidate number 5 has ....
....
....

Focus on ...
abbreviations

How would you abbreviate the phrases underlined?
a He's the <u>Managing Director</u> of the company. ........M.D.........
b Our profits rose this <u>September</u>. ....
c <u>Doctor</u> Martin leads our research team. ....
d The vehicle will travel at 180 <u>kilometres per hour</u>. ....
e The <u>administrative</u> staff are excellent. ....
f There are only a <u>limited number of opportunities</u>. ....

Learning tip

– Some common abbreviations use the first syllable(s) of a word (*freq* = frequently; *co* = company; *pop* = popular; *avail* = available). People sometimes use a full stop afterwards to show that it's an abbreviation.
– You can leave out unnecessary letters, particularly vowels. You can use an apostrophe or slash to make it clear that the word is abbreviated (dpt. = department; cont'd *or* cont/d = continued).
– For some common phrases we can use the first letters, with full stops if it is not clear that it is an abbreviation (*aka/AKA* or *a.k.a* = also known as).
– Add 's' for plurals (reps. = representatives; Ts = teachers, but T's = the teacher's).
– You can use symbols, e.g. *He's 50+.* means *He's over 50 years old.* Other useful symbols include:
  = (the same as); ∴ (therefore);
  ∵ (because); >> (much more than);
  → (which leads to).
Many people also develop their own forms of shorthand for notes:
Steak and roast pots. ✓✓✓ means *The steak and roast potatoes were very good*.

Did you know ...?

An acronym is a word made up from the first letters of the name of something. Acronyms are commonly used in the media and written in capital letters. For example:
AWOL (absent without leave = if somebody goes AWOL they have disappeared and you don't know where they are).
However, some acronyms are so common that most people don't know what they stand for any more and they are not written in capital letters (e.g. *radar, laser*). Another common shorthand term in the media is *24/7* to indicate 'all the time' (24 hours a day, 7 days a week).

Plan

6 You are a journalist for a celebrity magazine and are going to interview a well-known actor. Look at the questions you want to ask, then complete the exercises below.

> Question 1
> It's extraordinary you've been a movie actor for over 40 years. Is it true you've made over 200 films?
>
> Question 2
> It must be very difficult to keep fit when you're filming. How many hours a day do you exercise? I don't suppose you manage to get to the gym in the morning before you go onto the set, do you?
>
> Question 3
> Approximately 90 per cent of all your fans are children. Why do you think that is? Do you find it strange to be so popular with children when you mostly play frightening villains? For example, the foreign agent in the latest James Bond film.

a Full sentences are not necessary when writing notes. Which words in Question 1 could you omit?

----

b You can use dashes instead of full stops and commas and after question marks. Rewrite this note using a dash: *Fit? How many hrs a day exerc.?*

----

c Abbreviate these words and phrases: *over 40 years*; *difficult*; *in the morning*; *foreign*.

----

d You can emphasize important words by using CAPITAL LETTERS, <u>underlining</u>, and highlighting. Are there any words you will want to highlight?

----

e You can emphasize your emotions or attitude by punctuation (e.g. !!! ???). Give an example of where you will do that.

----

f Are there any symbols you will use to make your notes even shorter?

Write

7 Make a draft of your notes here.

Check

Now reread your notes and <u>underline</u> the correct alternative in these sentences. Make any changes that are necessary to your notes.

– The notes are *clear / not clear*.
– There *are some / aren't any* unnecessary words.
– I *understand / don't understand* my abbreviations.
– There are *some / no* parts that could be made clearer by highlighting.

E✗tra practice

1 You work for the Customer Services Department for this web company. A customer has accidentally been charged the full price for a camera instead of the reduced price and is now phoning to complain. What details do you think you will need to make a note of?

2 🔊 6 Listen to the conversation and make notes on a separate piece of paper.

3 a Look at the *Audioscript* on page 91. Underline the most important information. Is there anything missing from your notes?

   b Look at your notes again after an hour or two to see if you can still understand what you wrote.

Class bonus

Work in pairs or groups. Each pair or group should be A or B and write short notes for your situation.

Group A
Tell the Human Resources manager that a Mrs Scarlatti from the Leonardo Business School in Italy phoned and wants to arrange ten or more work placements for October. They want an answer very quickly.

Group B
Tell the Information Technology manager that your computer seems to be overheating and when you work on it for longer than two hours the screen freezes. You removed the cover and the computer then worked fine, but unfortunately you damaged something inside when trying to replace it. You are desperate. Ask for advice.

Give your notes to another group and ask them to write them out in full. Then read what they wrote. Was it what you meant?

Can-do checklist

Tick what you can do.

	Can do	Need more practice
I can use abbreviations effectively.		
I can listen and take short, clear notes.		
I can write simple messages.		

Unit 8
Here's what to do

go to Useful language p. 84

Get ready to write

○ Write answers to these questions.
a Which situations can you think of where you have to write instructions for someone?

----

b What do you think makes instructions effective?

A Instructions

Look at examples

1 Read these sets of instructions. Which set, 1, 2 or 3, is telling someone how to:

a use something? ☐
b get somewhere? ☐
c make something? ☐

2 Which one would you probably find:

a in an email to a friend? ☐
b in a rented flat/house? ☐
c on a website? ☐

1

►Welcome to Blog Set Up

To create a new blog:

1 Log into your account (Click here to register)
2 Choose a name for your blog
3 Choose a template design to determine the layout of your page
4 Choose a colour scheme
5 Add images and personalize your blog

2

🔥 GAS HEATER

First, make sure setting is on 0.

Then light pilot light by pressing PILOT LIGHT button (on left) and holding it down and pressing ignition button quickly.

When lit, keep PILOT LIGHT button down for 30 seconds and slowly release.

Next turn on HOT WATER and/or CENTRAL HEATING.

Finally, check all radiators are OPEN.

If any pipes spring leak, please turn off radiators and contact service engineer. (Phone no. on heater.)

3

When you come to the roundabout, you take the third exit and go straight on for about two kilometres. Stay on that road until you come to a post office on your left. That's where you need to turn off. As it's a bit complicated after that, I suggest you go into the post office and ask the way.

3 Compare the three sets of instructions in the areas below.

a format (e.g. numbering)

1: <u>uses a numbered list</u>

2: <u>uses separate sentences and words like First, Then, When, Finally etc.</u>

3: <u>writes sentences as part of a paragraph</u>

b punctuation

1: ....

2: ....

3: ....

c the use of articles *a(n)/the* and the subject pronoun *you*

1: ....

2: ....

3: ....

d politeness

1: ....

2: ....

3: ....

Learning tip

Instructions need to be clear and concise and convey the important information simply. We often use the imperative form (**Turn** *on the water.*) and sometimes we do not use the article (*Turn on* ~~**the water**~~.).

We can show the order in which things happen by using:
– numbers (*1, 2, 3…*)
– sequence expressions (*First, Secondly*)
– time words (*Monday, Tuesday…*).

Focus on …
clauses of time, condition and reason/purpose

When writing instructions we often use
– time clauses (**When** *you get there… /* **As soon as** *you can… /* **After** *you've finished…*)
– conditional clauses (*If any pipes leak…*)
– structures which give a reason or state a purpose: *To make/In order to make the sauce thicker, stir… So that there is enough to eat, make sure…*

Join these sentences beginning with the word in brackets. Make any necessary changes. Write in your notebook.

a Get the tickets. Post them to me. (*When*) *you get the tickets, post them to me.*

b Finish having dinner. Give me a ring. (*After*)

c It might be cold tonight. If so, light a fire. (*If*)

d You must finish the report. You'll need to stay at work late. (*In order to*)

e I don't want you to get lost. Please take a map. (*So that*)

f Get up at 6.00 tomorrow. Make me a cup of tea. (*When*)

Plan

4 🔘 **7** You are working for a summer school for foreign students. Head Office has just employed a new social organizer and has asked the Course Director to get someone to write an email to the organizer to explain what needs to be done and when. The Course Director has asked you to write the email. First, listen to the Course Director telling you what needs to be included and complete the timetable below.

SOCIAL ORGANIZER – Weekly Activity Sheet

MONDAY	TUESDAY	WEDNESDAY
Join with teachers to welcome new students.		
THURSDAY	**FRIDAY**	**SATURDAY**

Write

5 Now write your email to the new organizer. Use some of the expressions from the *Learning tip* and the *Focus on* sections. Begin:

The first thing you do on Monday is join with the teachers and …

Check

Reread your email and answer the following questions. Make any changes necessary to your answer.

– Have you included at least two instructions for each day of the week?
– Have you included all other necessary information? (You may want to check against the *Audioscript* on page 91.)
– Are your instructions clear?
– Is your style appropriate?

B Safety instructions

1 You have been asked to prepare a simple Fire Safety poster for your workplace, either on the computer or by hand. You need to make it clear and visually attractive.

Read this extract from a letter from a Health and Safety adviser. Highlight the key information.

The first priority if you discover a fire is to raise the alarm by operating the nearest alarm call point, then dial 999 and ask for the fire brigade. If it's just a small fire then you might be able to tackle it yourself by using some of the available appliances, but don't take any unnecessary risks. If you hear an alarm, obviously the first thing you do is to clear the building immediately by the quickest route, without stopping to collect personal belongings – instructions are posted in each room about the best route to take – and report to the assembly point. After that, it's very important you don't re-enter the building until the fire officers say it's safe to do so.

Plan

2 Decide whether you will make a numbered list or use sequence words.

3 This is a draft answer, which has not been edited. Read and answer the questions below.

a Which important information is missing?
b What changes could you make
   – to make the presentation clearer?
   – to make the order of information more logical?
   – to improve the style? (Look at phrases like *don't forget to, get out quick, don't bother*.)

FIRE INSTRUCTIONS
If you discover a fire
you must sound the alarm
don't forget to phone the fire brigade

If you hear the fire alarm
get out quick (quickest route) and
report to the assembly point
don't bother about personal belongings

Did you know …?

Public signs sometimes use the imperative.
KEEP FIRE DOOR SHUT!
However, *please* is often added to 'soften' the instruction.
PLEASE DRIVE CAREFULLY
When signs are used to prohibit something, we often prefer more polite forms of address.
~~DON'T WALK ON THE GRASS!~~ ✗
PLEASE DON'T WALK ON THE GRASS ✓
NO WALKING ON THE GRASS ✓
THANK YOU FOR NOT WALKING ON THE GRASS ✓ ✓

Write

4 Design your poster. Include the necessary information and make it as attractive as possible.

FIRE INSTRUCTIONS

If you discover

If you hear

Class bonus

1 Look at a local map and locate a place which is important to you (e.g. your friend's address).
2 Write an email or letter inviting another student to a party. Give directions how to get there, but do not give the street name or number.
3 Give the invitation to another student and ask them to follow your directions on the map. Can they find the correct location?

Check

5 Read it through and answer the questions in Exercise 3. Make any necessary changes.

Can-do checklist

Tick what you can do.

	Can do	Need more practice
I can write instructions saying how something works.		
I can use imperative forms to give instructions.		
I can present instructions clearly.		
I can use sequence words to show the order things happen.		

Unit 9
Let me write that down

Get ready to write

- Match the types of meetings with the definitions from the *Cambridge Advanced Learner's Dictionary*. Write the correct number (1–4) in the spaces.
  a annual general meeting (AGM) ......
  b video conferencing ......
  c round-table discussion ......
  d seminar ......

- Which meeting is the most formal? ....

- In which meetings are notes normally taken?

  ....

1 *noun* an occasion when a teacher or expert or a group of people meet to study and discuss something

2 *noun* when two or more people who are in different parts of the world can talk to each other and see each other on television screens

3 *noun* a meeting that happens once every year in which a company or other organization discusses the past year's activities and elects new officers

4 *noun* a meeting where people meet and talk in positions of equality

> go to Useful language p. 84

A Notes at a meeting

Look at examples

1 Look at notes 1–3 on the opposite page. Which notes:

a were written during a student seminar? ☐
b were written during a formal meeting? ☐
c were 'written up' (written in a complete and final form) after a meeting? ☐

2 Are these statements true (T) or false (F)?

a In 1 the writer has made some notes which will be written up later for a permanent record and possibly given to others. ......
b In 2 Sarah has made some notes to remind herself what she has just said. ......
c In 3 the writer has made some notes in a fairly organized fashion to remind him/her of what has been said. The notes may or may not be written up later. ......

3 In which note is personal opinion acceptable? ☐

4 Underline the correct alternative.

1: These notes have been written on a standard form. Each section has a *number / name* followed by a heading. The writer has used initials for the *names / numbers* of people and *symbols / abbreviations* to make the notes shorter.

2: In these notes the speaker's main observations are written under the heading *Key points / Action* . Under the heading *Key points / Action* the notes show what she thinks should happen as a result. There is *a lot of / little* punctuation.

3: These notes have been divided into two sections to show why the idea was good (pros/advantages) and why it wasn't as successful as the government had hoped (cons/disadvantages). There are *symbols / abbreviations* to make the points clearer and *punctuation / symbols* to show the writer's attitude. The main title, *A Shorter Working Week?*, indicates the *conclusion / topic* of the seminar. Under the Summary heading the writer gives *an example / a general conclusion* .

1

Minutes of **Johnson & Co** Finance Committee

Monday 12 June 2 pm

Present: *BC, DA, JG, KY, TR (Chair)*

1 Apologies
   WK BR.

2 Past Meetings
   Mins. 9 May agr./sign.

3 Matters Arising
   See agenda

4 Quarterly Report
   Manag. Accs. 4ᵗʰ qtr. DA ✓ new format

2

```
Sales and Marketing Report - Sarah Williamson

Key points:
• sales down 3.4%
• loss of market share in China
• possible new markets in Russia

Action:
Sales team to commission a market research
project in Russia
```

3

A SHORTER WORKING WEEK?
France : In 2000 Gov. made working week 35 hrs.
max (aver. over yr).
✓
The idea
-> Higher employ. (↑ wrk for ↑ people)
-> More leisure
-> Wkrs. less tired

✗
BUT
What often happened
-> Not higher employ. (emplyrs./-ees didn't want
*   small p-t jobs)*
-> More leisure but (in private sector) no ↑ in
*   money. Wkrs. unhappy!!!!*
-> Wkrs. more tired! - expctd. to work hrdr. in
*   ↓ hrs*

SUMMARY
An interest. exprmnt.????

5 **These are the written-up notes for 3. Complete the sentences.**

A shorter working week? (pros/cons)

In France, *(the) Government made (the) working week (a)*
maximum (of) 35 hours.

PROS
It would lead to:
• higher _____
• more _____
• _____

CONS
What often happened was
• _____
• _____
• _____

SUMMARY
_____

6 **What do you think the original notes for 2 looked like? Write them using abbreviations and symbols where possible.**

S&M Report : SW
* sales ↓3.4% _____
* mkt. _____
* new _____
Sales: mkt. _____

Did you know …?

Taking notes helps you concentrate, listen critically and understand what the speaker is saying. It also helps you remember it. Also, when you revise, personal notes are easier to absorb and remember than printed material. Most students use a combination of personal notes and printed material with sections highlighted.

Learning tip

Before you start
– Decide on how you will order the notes.
– If possible, organize your page so the main topics are clear.

While taking notes
– Don't try and write everything. Make sure you get the key facts, action points, etc.
– Try to separate facts, opinions and examples.
– Highlight key information where appropriate.
– Leave a blank space if you miss something completely so you can add it later.

Afterwards
– Read through your notes immediately and write them up as soon as possible.

Plan

7 Two senior colleagues are retiring. There is a meeting to plan their leaving party and your boss has asked you to write some notes on what is agreed. <u>Underline</u> the correct alternative.

a The aim of the notes is to *help you to concentrate on what you are listening to / provide a reminder of what is agreed*.

b They are for *your boss / you* to look at later.

c You will write them *in a formal style recording everything that is said / as abbreviated notes that you will write up after the meeting*.

8 These are some of the things that will be discussed. Put them in a logical order so you can take notes. The first one is done for you.

> TYPE OF EVENT
> ~~DATE~~ / ~~TIME~~
> GUEST LIST
> FOOD
> WHO TO ORGANIZE
> VENUE

DATE / TIME

Focus on ...
spelling of plural nouns

Look at the examples and write the plural of the nouns below.

pen → pens watch → watches (after **-s**, **-sh**, **-ch** and **-x**)
story → stories (when a noun ends in a consonant + **y**)

a speech ....*speeches*....   e journey _____
b taxi _____   f country _____
c address _____   g month _____
d box _____   h baby _____

Write

9 🔊 **18** Listen to the discussion and take notes under your headings. Use abbreviations and symbols where appropriate.

Check

Read your notes. Are they clear to you? If necessary, listen again or look at the *Audioscript* on pages 91 and 92 and check you have included the key information under each heading. Add anything you have missed or change anything you misunderstood the first time you heard it.

E✗tra practice

This is a written-up version of the notes but there are mistakes in it. Also the sections have been jumbled up. Rewrite it on a separate piece of paper, correcting the mistakes and putting the sections in a more logical order.

Guest list
• Present staff but no partners.

Venue
• Outside the main reception area.

Date/time
• The first Friday at lunch time.

Who to organize
• Tom and his wife.

LEAVING PARTY

Food
• Our own catering staff.

Type of event
• A dinner party. ? will probably make a speech.

B Notes at a seminar

Plan

1 **You are taking part in a college seminar on mass tourism. Look at the pictures. Write an example of one of the things that might be said.**

----

2 **You are going to take some notes at the seminar. Write these in the most likely place below:**

> ✗ *(disadvantages)*   *WHAT NEEDS TO BE DONE*   ✓ *(advantages)*
> *MASS TOURISM*

MAIN HEADING: _____

SUBHEADING 1: _____

SUBHEADING 2: _____

CONCLUDING HEADING: _____

Write

3 🔊**9** **Listen to the discussion and make notes of the key points under each heading above. There is no need to indicate who said what.**

Check

Read your notes and answer the following questions. Make any changes that are necessary to your notes.

– Do you understand them?
– Have you included only the most important points under each heading? Is there anything missing? (Listen again or read the *Audioscript* on page 92 to check.)
– Have you used either bullet points or a numbering system?
– Have you used abbreviations and/or symbols?
– Have you used your own words as far as possible?

Class bonus

1 Work in groups. Agree on the most important point or points in the seminar under each heading.
2 Make a summary of these points using a maximum of 20 words.
3 One person from each group should use the summary to present their points to the other groups. (Begin: *In our view, the most important points that came up in the seminar were …*)
4 Compare the summaries.

Can-do checklist

Tick what you can do.

	Can do	Need more practice
I can select the most important information.		
I can make notes while participating in a meeting/seminar.		
I can lay out and organize notes logically and clearly.		
I can use abbreviations and symbols appropriately in notes.		
I can write up notes clearly.		

Unit 10
Our sincere apologies

Get ready to write

○ 🎧 **10** Listen to two situations (a and b). Where are they?

a .... b ....

○ Why do people sometimes write letters of complaint after being in these places?

a ....

b ....

go to Useful language pp. 84–5

A Letter of complaint

Look at an example

1 **This letter is in jumbled order. Write the correct order.**

..E.. ....

....

2 **Which sentence is correct, a or b?**

a MAGIradio is writing a formal letter of complaint to Digital Supplies. ☐

b Digital Supplies is writing a letter of apology for supplying damaged radios. ☐

3 **What does the person writing the letter want to happen?**

....

....

4 **Match the letters A–I with these descriptions.**

subject line ..B..
reference to previous contact ......
name and title ......
formal ending ......
explanation of the problem ......
address of person receiving the letter ......
formal greeting ......
the company sending the letter and the date it was written ......
explanation of what is needed ......

A   Yours sincerely

B   Digital radio supplies: Orders TF261 and ZH 679

C   We trust that this situation does not indicate a decline in your service standards and that the radios will be replaced immediately.

D   Dear Mr Shipwell

E   **MAGIradio**   14 Greenwood Park Guildford GU3 7PH

                                         15 April 20…

F   With order number TF261, five of the radios we ordered were damaged on arrival and with order number ZH 679, two were missing from our order of 30. Please note that we have still not received replacements for the damaged radios.

G   Maria Greco
Sales and Marketing Director

H   We have been regular customers of Digital Supplies for some years and have been generally satisfied with the service you offer. However, the last two deliveries have proved very unsatisfactory.

I   Tom Shipwell
Digital Supplies
Hills Business Park
Cambridge
CS7 H90

5 <u>Underline</u> a polite, formal expression in the letter which has a similar meaning to these.

  a In the main we've been pretty pleased with what you do for us.
  b You've really messed up with the last two lots of stuff you sent us.
  c … broken when they got here.
  d You still haven't sent us new ones.
  e I hope this doesn't mean that you're not as good as you used to be.

6 **Ms Jamali is the customer services representative at Sunlight Holidays. She has written this email to apologize to Mr Sarit, one of her regular clients. Read the email and decide what Ms Jamali is apologizing for.**

7 **Ms Jamali knows Mr Sarit quite well and they have a friendly relationship. <u>Underline</u> the correct alternative for an *informal* email.**

Thank you for your letter / <u>Thanks for your note</u> of 15th November.

I'm really sorry / I was extremely concerned to hear that there was no driver or other member of staff to meet you at the airport when you flew in from Thailand last Thursday. *I've checked it out / I have looked into the matter very closely* and found that this was entirely our fault and due to some poor communications internally. *However, I would like to assure you / I'm sure you understand* that this is not typical of how our company operates.

I hope you will accept our apologies for the inconvenience caused / I'm really sorry about the mix-up and hope *that it won't stop you working with us! / you will continue to work with us in the future.*

Plan

8 **Recently, you booked your staff into a hotel you have used for a number of years, but on this occasion there were some problems. You are going to write a letter of complaint and ask for a refund. Read an extract from the itinerary, the fax you originally sent and some notes you have made. Although you and your staff have used the hotel, you have never met the hotel manager. What style will you write in?**

ITINERARY

Thursday 14th July. Overnight stay at Chequers Hotel, Ely.

Friday 15th. Attend 'New Directions' Conference at Ely Conference Centre

---

FAX   30th June

FROM: Management International
TO: Hotel Manager, Chequers Hotel

I would like to reserve single rooms for eight of our staff for the night of 14th July. We will be arriving at 2 pm and will need three car parking spaces. We also request adjoining rooms because our team have to work together to prepare for a conference they are attending. Please note that all rooms should be non-smoking.

Problems with hotel
· no parking spaces – had to park at nearby public car park. Very expensive!!!
· no adjoining rooms – everyone on different floor AND lift out of order!
· rooms NOT ready at 2.00 pm
· 2 rooms not prop. cleaned; 1 air con. not working; 1 placed on smkng. corridor.
· 'short-staffed' 'nothing we can do' !!! – Receptionist rude.

9 **Look again at the notes you made on page 51. The problems your staff had can be divided into three topics. Write the topics here.**

Problem 1 _____

Problem 2 _____

Problem 3 _____

10 **Put these paragraph topics in the best order for your letter.**

a Asking for a refund ☐
b Giving the background to the letter ☐
c The reaction of the receptionist ☐
d Saying why you're writing 1
e Problem 1 ☐
f Problem 2 ☐
g Problem 3 ☐

Focus on …

participle clauses

Participle clauses can be used in writing to make sentences shorter.

On complaining, my staff were told that your hotel was short-staffed. (= *When they complained*)

Having been promised reserved parking spaces, we were surprised to find there were none. (= *Since we had been promised*)

Note that

– present and perfect participles (**On complaining**… / **Having complained**…) are used for actions/ situations at the same time or in a sequence.
– past participles (*Having been* **promised**…) are used for passive sentences.
– a participle clause must have the same subject as the verb in the main clause (*On complaining, / When* **my staff** *complained*, **they** *(my staff) were told*…).

In your notebook, rewrite the sentences below using a participle clause. Begin with the word(s) in brackets.

a As soon as he reached the door, he heard the telephone ring. (*On*) *reaching the door, he heard the telephone ring.*
b He hadn't had any exercise all day so he felt like going for a walk. (*Not having*)
c He couldn't afford to give the job up even though he hated it. (*While hating*)
d Peter spent all day in bed because he was ill. (*Being*)
e I got married since I saw you last. (*Since last seeing*)
f As Klara has lived in Warsaw all her life, she knows the city very well. (*Having*)
g The car turned right at the crossroads and went north. (*Turning*)
h As the film was directed by an artist, it was very beautiful to look at. (*Having*)

Learning tip

When writing a letter of complaint to a senior person, write a formal letter, not an email.
– Be polite, respectful and as positive as possible.
– Explain the situation clearly.
– Don't be emotional and aggressive. This can make the other person react negatively.
– Keep the letter as short as possible and to the point.
– Ask for an early reply or make it clear what you want to happen.

Did you know …?

When a new law concerning airline passengers' rights came into effect in 2006, the number of written complaints trebled. The most common causes of complaints were: cancellations, delays and mishandled bags.

Write

11 **Write a draft of your letter in about 250 words.**

Check

Read your letter and check to make sure:

– you have explained the situation (i.e. that you had made a group booking)
– you make it clear what you were promised and in what way the promises were broken
– you have said what happened when you complained
– you have said what you want to happen as a result and why
– you are polite and firm but not aggressive
– your spelling is correct.

Make any changes that are necessary.

B Letter of apology

1 **🔊 11 You work for a company that runs seminars and workshops for business people. Rick Hayden, a regular client, has left a telephone message on your answerphone to complain about a mix-up over a booking. Your colleague made some notes on the message but there are five mistakes. Listen to the message and correct the notes.**

Rick phoned — tried to book 3 mgrs. on to Communications wkshp. — booking a bit late but told no problem. Received email conf, — deposit accpt'd. On arrival, mgrs. told: no booking made/ no places left. Rick not happy — says 2ⁿᵈ time this has happened.

Plan

2 **You are going to write an email to Rick to apologize for the mix-up. Read this extract from an email you have received from the organizer of the seminar. Decide**

- what you are going to say in reply
- the number of paragraphs you need and what you will say in each
- the style you will use.

Don't know who first took the call from Rick. The problem was we could only take 25 on the workshop and over 50 applied. Let's run the workshop again next month. Offer him 50% discount?

Write

3 **Write your email in about 200 words.**

Check

Read your email and check to make sure:

- you have explained how the misunderstanding occurred
- you have said what you can offer Rick
- the sentences are clear and the organization of the paragraphs is logical
- the style you are writing in is appropriate for Rick in this context
- the letter will have the effect you want on Rick.

Make any changes that are necessary.

Class bonus

Work with a group of other students. You have just returned from a round-the-world trip organized by a travel agent. Unfortunately, a lot of things went wrong.

1 Brainstorm all the things that went wrong.

2 One of you is the agent, the others are the people who want to complain. Role play a visit to the agent and make your complaints.

3 Now, as a group, decide on the most important issues and write a formal letter of complaint to the head office of the travel agent.

Can-do checklist

Tick what you can do.

	Can do	Need more practice
I can write a letter of complaint.		
I can write a letter/email of apology.		
I can decide when to use formal/informal language.		

Get ready to write

- Which of these (a–c) are important when you travel for work or study?
- Which of them are important when you travel on holiday?
- How important is it to have everything planned and organized in advance when you travel?

a

ITINERARY
28th July

8.30	Leave hostel.
9.40	Arrive at museum

b

Roma Grand Hotel

Dear Sir,

This is to comfirm your hotel booking with us for your stay in Rome.
We hope you will enjoy visiting the wonderful city.

c

GLOBAL INTERNATIONAL SCHOOL

go to Useful language p. 85

A Email about travel plans

Look at examples

1 Read these emails. How do you think the writers know each other?

1

Dear Mr Li

I'm visiting the US in July and plan to be in Los Angeles on the 11th. Would it be possible for us to meet and discuss future cooperation?

Sincerely
Juan Ramos

2

Dear Mr Ramos

I'm delighted to hear that you will be coming to LA. I really look forward to seeing you again. If you would like to write me and tell me your flight number and time of arrival, I could meet you at the airport and take you to your hotel.

Best regards

Li Yanchun

3

Dear Mr Li

Thank you very much for offering to meet me at the airport. It's very kind of you. My schedule is as follows: I'm arriving at LA International Airport on flight BA 693 at 14.30 and staying at the Radisson Hotel.

It would be very helpful if you were able to meet me at the airport, but if it's too much trouble, don't worry as I can easily get a taxi.

I look forward to meeting you again and discussing our plans with you.

Sincerely
Juan Ramos

2 <u>Underline</u> the correct alternative.

a They *are / are not* complete strangers.

b They *are / are not* close friends.

c They write to each other *informally / politely / very formally* .

3 **Which email (1, 2, or 3) is**

a making an offer? _2_

b accepting an offer? _____

c making a request? _____

4 <u>Underline</u> the polite phrases in each email (e.g. *Would it be possible...?*).

5 (Circle) the verb forms they use to talk about their travel plans (e.g. *I'm visiting*).

Did you know ...?

There are far fewer differences between standard American and standard British English than many people think. However, there are some small differences in grammar, spelling and vocabulary, for example in the use of prepositions:

British English	**American English**
Write to me *and tell me your flight number.*	***Write me*** *and tell me your flight number.*
Tom will **meet the manager**.	*Tom will* **meet with the manager**.
We'll be in Beijing **on Thursday**. *The office is closed* **at the weekend**.	*We'll be in Beijing* **Thursday**. *The office is closed* **on the weekend**.

Plan

6 🔊 **12 You are going to Moscow on business. Listen to a message left on your answerphone by Mr Zhirkov, one of the people involved in the deal. Make notes on what he says.**

7 Look at this itinerary made by your assistant after discussions with you. You have made some comments on it. Which of Mr Zhirkov's suggestions do you not agree with?

Learning tip

When you write an itinerary leave out less important words (e.g. the subject *you*, articles, some verbs: ~~You have a~~ meeting with ~~Ms~~ Raisa Petrova → Meeting with Raisa Petrova).

ITINERARY: VISIT TO MOSCOW (Capital Enterprises)

DATE: Monday 4th August

16.30	Arrive at Sheremetyevo Airport (KLM 1010). Taxi to Holiday Inn Hotel. (Taxi booked. Contact details attached.)
19.30	Dinner in hotel with Andrei Zhirkov (Managing Director, Capital Enterprises).

Thank Zhirkov but tell him 'no'. Will want to check into the hotel

I'll get his mobile no. and phone him if I'm delayed.

Tuesday 5th August

09.00	Taxi from hotel to Alma Bank. (journey time approx. 10 mins. Details attached.)
09.30-10.30	Meeting with Ms Raisa Petrova (General Manager).
10.30	Walk to Capital Enterprises (approx. 2 mins walk — map attached).
11.00-13.00	Meet Mr Zhirkov at reception. Tour of company.
13.00-14.00	Lunch with staff in company cafeteria???
14.00→	Discussions with Mr Zhirkov.
20.05	Depart Sheremetyevo Airport (KLM 2450).

??? — I'll make sure this is OK with Zhirkov

Yes, this was his idea

I'll book a taxi for the airport when I'm there.

8 You are going to email Mr Zhirkov and give him some idea of your plans for Monday and Tuesday. Decide on how many paragraphs you need and the topic of each paragraph. Start by responding to his answerphone message.

EXAMPLE

Paragraph 1: Thank Mr Zhirkov but say 'no'

Paragraph 2: ....

etc.

9 These are possible sentence openings. Tick ✓ any of them you want to use and write the paragraph number.

Thank you very much for ☐

Rather than coming to the company on Monday evening, can I suggest ☐

The next morning, before coming to Capital Enterprises ☐

I think we agreed that before starting our discussions ☐

My plane home leaves at 8.05 but ☐

Focus on ...

talking about future travel plans

going to (intentions/predictions)

present continuous (personal arrangements already made)

present simple (public timetables/programmes)

future continuous (future events already arranged for the whole period)

likely to (probably); *bound to* (certainly); *due to* (expected at a certain time)

Underline the most natural form below.

a *I'm visiting* / I visit New York next week. According to my itinerary, *I'll be staying* / I stay at the Hyatt, which is quite near to you, so any chance of us meeting?

b It'd be great to see you. I'll send you the address of my hotel when I know where *I'm staying* / I stay.

c Have you decided what *you do* / *you're going to do* when you get here?

d I'm not sure what time the restaurant *opens* / *is going to open*. About 7.00, I think.

e My plane's *due to arrive* / *arriving* at about 6.00 – I hope it's on time.

f Hi Juan! Just a quick text. The plane's delayed. I think *I'm going to arrive* / *I'm arriving* late for the meeting

g The airport bus is *likely to be* / *bound to be* full – it always is.

---

10 You have met Mr Zhirkov once before and are going to write in a polite but friendly style. The opening paragraph below is too informal and casual. Rewrite it in a more appropriate style.

Re 4th at 4.30 Moscow – thanks for the offer. I've already got a taxi booked to take me to the hotel – my assistant fixed it up – so don't bother. Anyway, I'll need a rest before we meet.

Begin:

Thank you very much for your kind offer to meet me at the airport on ......

Write

11 Write a draft of your email in 150–200 words.

Check

Check to make sure:

– you have thanked Mr Zhirkov for his offer

– you have asked for his mobile phone number

– you have told him you will make your own travel arrangements to the airport

– you have the correct level of politeness

– you have used the correct verb forms to talk about travel plans.

Make any changes that are necessary.

B Itinerary

Plan

1 Mitsuko is based in the UK and arranges tours of Europe for Japanese students. She is organizing a ten-day tour of France with the help of Laurent, a French travel agent. If you could visit France, which places would you go to and what would you want to do? Write your ideas here.

....

....

2 🔊 **13** **Listen to Mitsuko talk to Laurent. Tick ✓ any of your ideas that are mentioned.**

3 Listen again and complete the gaps in this itinerary. Write *TBA* after something not yet arranged.

10-DAY CULTURE AND HISTORY TOUR OF FRANCE

March 1st
am
Eurostar London-Paris
Depart ....
Arrive ....
Coach to ....
pm
.... (e.g. Eiffel Tower, Notre Dame)

March 2nd–5th
am
.... (TBA)
pm
.... (e.g. Louvre, Versailles)

March 6th
am
TGV ....
Coach ....
pm
....

March 7th–8th
Coach tour of .... (e.g. ....)
.... (TBA)

March 9th
.... Monaco.
(Selected lectures at ....)

March 10th
....
Return to the UK

Write

4 Mitsuko has an English colleague who helps her with the tours. Write an email from Mitsuko to the colleague in about 180 words giving an outline of the tour so far. Begin: *I've spoken to the French travel agent and …*

Check

Look at the *Audioscript* on page 93 and check that you have included the most important information.

Class bonus

Work in groups. You are going to prepare an itinerary for an important foreign visitor who is coming to visit your town. Decide:
– who the person is, the length of stay and the purpose of the visit
– where the person will stay
– what visits/meetings you will organize
– who will meet and escort the person at different times
– whether you will organize some spare-time activities (e.g. restaurants, theatres) or leave spare time free.
Plan your itinerary.

Can-do checklist

Tick what you can do.

	Can do	Need more practice
I can write a formal email about travel plans.		
I can write in a polite but friendly style.		
I can use future forms to talk about travel plans.		
I can write an itinerary.		

Unit 12
Can you write a report?

Get ready to write

○ Sometimes students and recent graduates take an 'internship' (they work in a real company as part of their training for a skilled job but get little or no pay). Are internships common in your country?

○ Write one advantage for the student/graduate.

○ Write one advantage for the company.

----

go to Useful language p. 85

A Report

Look at an example

1 Read this report. Can you guess:

a who has commissioned the report and why?

    ----

b who will read the report?

    ----

2 Look at the structure of the report and write 1–4 to show the correct order.

CONCLUSION	☐
TITLE	1
MAIN SECTION	☐
INTRODUCTION	☐

ELECTRO Mobiles
The best in mobile phone technology

REPORT ON PROPOSED INTERNSHIP PROGRAMME

Introduction
The purpose of this report is to consider the advantages and disadvantages of recruiting interns into the company. I have discussed the issue with a number of companies who accept interns and interviewed local colleges and universities who would wish to collaborate with us.

Advantages
The main advantages are:
1 lower recruitment and labour costs
2 we have the opportunity to train highly motivated graduates
3 we benefit from fresh, new ideas
4 we establish a pool of potential employees who have demonstrated their abilities
5 it provides good publicity for our company.

Disadvantages
Most employers I interviewed agreed that the biggest disadvantages of an internship programme are:
1 the extra workload it places on managers to train and monitor interns
2 some interns lose motivation if they realize there is no prospect of full employment when the programme finishes.

Conclusion and recommendation
Clearly, there are risks attached to setting up an internship programme but on the whole everyone agrees that the benefits would far outweigh the disadvantages and that we should trial a scheme for a limited period.

3 Under which heading does the writer talk about

a why internships would be good for the company?
......Advantages......

b the aims of the report?
----

c how the benefits are greater than the risks?
----

d how the information was obtained?
----

e how internships could cause problems for the company?
----

4 Tick ✓ the things which are used to make the report easier to read.

bullet points ☐   numbers ☐
underlining ☐   headings ☐

5 Which of these best describe the style? Tick ✓ one or more of the boxes.

impersonal and formal ☐
personal and informal ☐
clear and neutral ☐
balanced, showing positive and negative points fairly ☐

6 Match these phrases from the report with the descriptions.

a *on the whole*   1 Stating the aim
b *clearly*   2 Saying what people said
c *we should*   3 Showing your attitude indirectly
d *everyone agrees that*
e *the purpose of …*   4 Making a generalization
  is to…   5 Recommending

7 Which description (1–5) in Exercise 6 best matches these words and phrases commonly used in reports?

hopefully ..3..
in the main ......
(This report) is intended to ......
all things considered ......
the majority (of staff) felt that ......
we have no hesitation in proposing ......
there is little doubt that ......

Plan

8 🔊 114 A local university is worried that its current sports facilities might not meet the needs of students and staff. You have been asked to write a short report on the situation and suggest appropriate action to take. Listen to comments from staff and students and make notes on points to use in your report.

9 Tick ✓ which of these you will recommend.

no action needed ☐
major investment ☐
minor improvements ☐
set up a committee to make proposals ☐
seek external funding ☐

10 Which of these would make good headings for the main body of the report?

Advantages ☐
Disadvantages ☐
The way forward ☐
Future facilities ☐
Problems ☐
Strengths and limitations ☐
Current facilities ☐
Raising money ☐
Overview ☐
Introduction ☐
Interviews ☐

11 Which paragraph plan is the most suitable?

a	b	c
Introduction	Introduction	Interviews
Disadvantages	Current facilities	Problems
Advantages	Strengths and	Future facilities
The way forward	limitations	Raising money
	Recommendations	

12 Decide on your layout. How will you list points? How will you highlight headings?

Learning tip

Before you write a report, think carefully about its aim, collect the data and organize it carefully.
In the report, state the aim clearly and lay the report out in a way that makes it easy to read with simple headings, bullet points or numbers for a list etc.
Often busy readers will only read the conclusion/ recommendations, so make this section as clear and concise as possible.

Focus on ...
writing in a neutral style

1 These phrases could be used to open each paragraph. Write them in a more neutral style suitable for a report.

a In this report I want to …
The main aims _of this report are to_

b To prepare for this report I interviewed …
In order to .... I ....
As preparation .... , I ....

c Right now …
At ....

d The people I spoke to liked the gym but most of them said the rest of the facilities were completely useless.
While the people I .... ,
most felt that ....

e I really feel the committee ought to …
In my ....

2 Complete the sentences with the verbs in the correct form to make a possible final paragraph.

| report | make | need | raise | ~~consist~~ | set up | suggest |

A committee ...._consisting_.... of students and staff should be .... to draw up a plan for future developments and .... to the Principal. This committee should .... proposals for improvements over the next five years and .... methods of .... the funds which ....

Write

13 Write a draft of your report.

Check

Check to make sure:

- all the information is relevant
- you have avoided repetition
- positive and negative points are balanced
- different viewpoints are represented fairly
- your report is organized so that it is easy to read (e.g. there are headings/subheadings, the points are numbered or have bullet points)
- your style is clear and neutral and you have avoided personal comment
- you have avoided contractions, abbreviations, idioms and colloquial expressions.

Make any changes that are necessary to your answer.

B Editing reports

1 **You have been asked to write up these notes in the form of a report. The report should have the following title:**
REPORT ON MAIN CURRENT ENVIRONMENTAL ISSUES FACING OUR COUNTRY
Read the notes and answer these questions.

a What are the three main problems?
....
....
....

b What successes have there been?
....

c Is enough being done to improve the situation?
....

air pollution – (too many old vehicles) big problem
→ disease/respiratory problems (recent controls have slightly improved air quality but..)

water – on av. we use 300 ltrs. a day/ recently population ↑↑ → far more water taken from ground than replaced by rainfall √√√ water companies replacing piping to reduce leaks

tourism – too many! (sites of natural beauty being destroyed) √ govern. launched eco-tourism programme wants tourists to respect environ.

Last few years economy → but too little protection for environ. Some successes but more to be done. Dangers to human health/life in gen.

Did you know ...?

According to scientists, the world will be at least three degrees warmer by the end of the century. Extra heat causes even more greenhouse gases.

2 Read the unedited report on the right and answer the questions below.

a Is there a clear overall structure to the report?
b Has the writer used subheadings below the main headings?
c Is there an introduction and a conclusion?
d Is the style always clear and neutral, and appropriate for a report?
e Has the writer avoided contractions (e.g. *we'd*), note-like phrases and abbreviations?
f Can you find at least one example of incorrect grammar and two examples of incorrect punctuation and spelling?

3 Now write an improved version of the report. Remember to include an introduction and a conclusion.

4 Check your report. Use the questions in Exercise 2 to help you.

Main problems

1 Air polution
Air polution – serious problem in all the big cities, not just ours – mainly because of exhuast fumes, it is a major cause of disease and respiratory probs.

2 Water
The average citizen in our lovely country uses 300 ltrs. a day, and now that there are more us here than there used to be, we're taking far more water from the ground than goes back in when it rains

3 Tourism
because of the number of tourists visiting our country they are destroying sights of nat. beauty

Successes

1 The air quality's getting a bit better thanks to the recent controls on vehicles

2 The water companies replaceing pipes to reduce the no. of water leaks.

3 The government has launched an eco-tourism programme which aim to get tourists to respect environ.

Class bonus

Work in groups of four.
1 What are the main environmental problems in your country? Make a list of as many as you can think of.
2 For each of the problems make notes under the following headings:
– what the problem is and the effect it is having
– the long-term dangers
– what is being done
– what needs to be done
3 Each person in the group should be responsible for a section of the report and write a paragraph.
4 Show each other your paragraphs and make the style and format consistent.
5 Write or word-process a neat version with a heading.
6 Show your report to other groups or put it on the wall to read. Do you all agree on what needs to be done?

Can-do checklist

Tick what you can do.

	Can do	Need more practice
I can write a well-structured report based on interviews.		
I can write in an appropriate neutral style for a report.		
I can write a report based on notes.		
I can improve an unedited text.		

Get ready to write

- Do you know who painted these
Impressionist paintings? Which one is by:
Pierre-Auguste Renoir (1841–1919)? ☐
Camille Pissarro (1830–1903)? ☐
Claude Monet (1840–1926)? ☐

a   b   c

- Do you like this style of painting?
Why? / Why not?

go to Useful language p. 85

A Summarizing key points

Look at an example

1 Ildiko is attending a Cultural Studies course
in Cape Town. She loves art and has written a
summary of Impressionism. Read her summary.

> Impressionism was a style of painting that
> *developed chiefly in France* (a) during the late
> 19th century. It was an attempt to create the
> *general impression of what we see* (b) *through
> effects of light and colour* (c). Among the most
> important Impressionist painters were Monet,
> Renoir and Pissarro. They used short brush-
> strokes of *pure and unmixed colour* (d) and took
> the act of painting *out of the studio into the real
> world* (e).

2 Read the sources 1–3, then look again at
phrases a–e in Ildiko's summary. Where did
Ildiko find each piece of information? Write
the source 1–3 and underline the phrase or
phrases used. More than one source may have
been used.

a _2_   b _____   c _____   d _____   e _____

1

Impressionism: A style of painting that uses colour to show
the effects of light on the visible world and to suggest atmosphere
rather than showing exact details.

2

Impressionism <u>developed in France</u> during the
1870s through the works of Claude Monet, Pierre
Auguste Renoir and Camille Pissarro, although
its <u>influence extended</u> to painters such as
Winslow Homer in <u>the United States</u>. Previously,
portraits and even landscapes had been painted
indoors, but the Impressionists found that they
could capture the effects of sunlight by painting
outdoors. From the 1880s several artists, like
Vincent Van Gogh and Paul Gauguin, sometimes
known as Post-Impressionists, started to develop
different ideas about colour and form.

3

Impressionist techniques

- Short visible brushstrokes of paint are used to capture
the essence of the subject.
- Changes in natural light are emphasized. Close attention
is paid to the reflection of colours from object to object.
- Colours are put side by side with as little mixing as
possible.

3 <u>Underline</u> the correct answer.

a The last sentence in source 2 has been left out of Ildiko's summary because it is not *interesting / relevant*.

b Ildiko says 'chiefly' in phrase a because *this style of painting also influenced painters in the United States / she is not sure it only influenced painters in France*.

Plan

4 You are studying film and researching the history of horror films. You need to write a summary about this type of film to help you later when you revise. Look at these extracts from two different sources about the history of horror films and highlight the most important information. Then make some notes of the key points under these headings:

What are horror films and why do we like them?
The 1930s
The 1950s

A

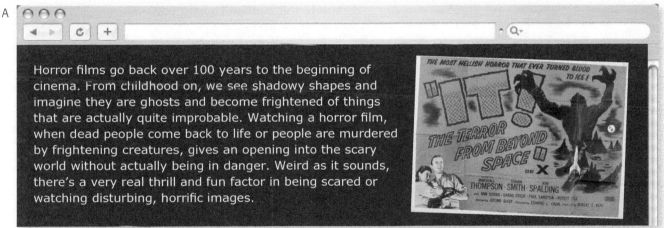

Horror films go back over 100 years to the beginning of cinema. From childhood on, we see shadowy shapes and imagine they are ghosts and become frightened of things that are actually quite improbable. Watching a horror film, when dead people come back to life or people are murdered by frightening creatures, gives an opening into the scary world without actually being in danger. Weird as it sounds, there's a very real thrill and fun factor in being scared or watching disturbing, horrific images.

B

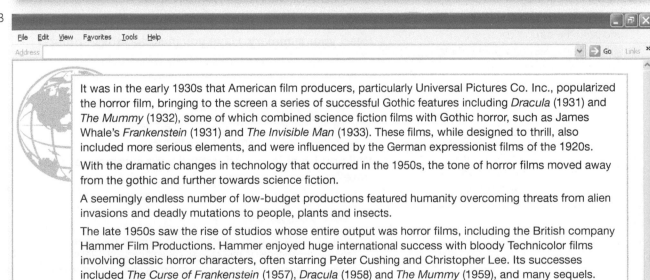

It was in the early 1930s that American film producers, particularly Universal Pictures Co. Inc., popularized the horror film, bringing to the screen a series of successful Gothic features including *Dracula* (1931) and *The Mummy* (1932), some of which combined science fiction films with Gothic horror, such as James Whale's *Frankenstein* (1931) and *The Invisible Man* (1933). These films, while designed to thrill, also included more serious elements, and were influenced by the German expressionist films of the 1920s.

With the dramatic changes in technology that occurred in the 1950s, the tone of horror films moved away from the gothic and further towards science fiction.

A seemingly endless number of low-budget productions featured humanity overcoming threats from alien invasions and deadly mutations to people, plants and insects.

The late 1950s saw the rise of studios whose entire output was horror films, including the British company Hammer Film Productions. Hammer enjoyed huge international success with bloody Technicolor films involving classic horror characters, often starring Peter Cushing and Christopher Lee. Its successes included *The Curse of Frankenstein* (1957), *Dracula* (1958) and *The Mummy* (1959), and many sequels.

5 Below are two extracts from reviews of the films that will be used as examples in your summary. Do you know the films? If so, do you agree with the opinions?

Psycho directed by Alfred Hitchcock
Despite effective moments of fright, it has a childish plot and script, and its interest is that of a tremendously successful confidence trick, made for very little money by a TV crew.

The Blair Witch Project is an extraordinarily effective horror film, knows this and uses it. It has no fancy special effects or digital monsters, but its characters get lost in the woods, hear noises in the night and find disturbing stick figures hanging from trees.

6 15 Now listen to a podcast about the films and write *T* (true) or *F* (false) next to these statements.

1 *Psycho* and *The Blair Witch Project* illustrate the horror film genre. __T__
2 All the critics agree that *Psycho* is a psychological thriller. ......
3 It is about a woman who stole some money and is on the run. ......
4 The woman is staying in a busy hotel. ......
5 Norman Bates is a friend of hers. ......
6 There is a horrific murder. ......
7 In *The Blair Witch Project* three film students are making a film about a local legend. ......
8 They never return from the woods. ......
9 This horror film is full of special effects. ......

Focus on ...
defining relative clauses

Complete the sentences with *who, which, that, where, when* or *whose.*
a They are films in ......*which*...... frightening things happen.
b Earlier films were ones .... mixed in science fiction and expressionist films.
c The British made films .... main characters were creatures like Dracula.
d It was a time .... many horror films were made.
e *Psycho* is about a woman .... is on the run.
f She has stolen money from the place .... she works.
g *The Blair Witch Project* is about three students .... make a film about a local legend.
h These are the two films .... best illustrate the genre in recent years.

Write

7 Write your summary in about 200 words. You can complete this outline to help you.

We have been thrilled by .... since ....
They allow us to be .... In the early 1930s there were .... and ones which ....
However, in the 1950s .... while the British .... Since then two films ....
Most critics agree that *Psycho* is .... , although one critic .... It is about .... *The Blair Witch Project* is about .... According to one critic, ...

Check

Read your summary. Have you included these points?

– what happens in horror films and why we like them
– how the horror films in the 1950s were different from those in the 1930s
– in what way *Psycho* was different
– what *Psycho* and *The Blair Witch Project* were about
– why *The Blair Witch Project* was effective.

Will you be able to understand your summary at a later date?

Did you know ...?

In 1998, director Gus van Sant made a frame-by-frame remake of *Psycho*. He hoped that the colour film and improved sound would make the story popular with modern audiences.

E X tra practice

1 You are researching race relations and have been asked to write a brief summary comparing the lives of Dr Martin Luther King, Jr and Nelson Mandela. What sort of information do you think you will include?

2 🔊 **16** Read these extracts and listen to the radio news items. Make notes of the points you will include in your summary.

Dr Martin Luther King, Jr (1929–68). Black minister for a branch of the Christian church and civil rights campaigner, born in Atlanta, GA. He became a leader of the civil rights movement, known for his policy of passive resistance and his skill at public speaking. In 1964 he received the Nobel Peace Prize. His greatest success came in challenging the segregation laws of the South. He was assassinated in Memphis, Tennessee on 9 April 1968.

Nelson Mandela (1918–). South African statesman and president (1994–1999), born in Transkei, South Africa. He was a lawyer in Johannesburg, then joined the African National Congress (ANC) in 1944 and became its leader. For the next 20 years he directed a campaign of defiance against the racist policies of the government. In 1964 he was sentenced to imprisonment for political offences and was not released until 1990. In 1991 he became president of the ANC and was closely involved in negotiations with President de Klerk, which led to South Africa's first all-race elections in 1994. In 1993 both he and de Klerk shared the Nobel Peace Prize. Mandela is now retired and an elder statesman who continues to voice his opinion on topical issues.

3 Write your summary in about 200 words.

4 Edit your answer, checking the grammar, punctuation and spelling.

Class bonus

1 You are going to find some information about your country and bring it to class. As a class choose one of these general topics:
   – a famous person
   – an important historical event
   – something in the news.

2 Each student should decide separately on who or what they will find out about.

3 Bring the information to class, together with some photographs if possible.

4 Work in groups and show and tell each other what you have brought. Other students should take notes of the most important points.

5 Write a short summary of one of the presentations, making comparisons and contrasts where appropriate.

Can-do checklist

Tick what you can do.

	Can do	Need more practice
I can make notes of key information in a text.		
I can make a summary of key information for review/revision.		
I can use relative clauses correctly in descriptions.		

Unit 14
Handing in a good essay

Get ready to write

- Are these statements true (T) or false (F) for you?
  I am a vegetarian. ......
  I think it's important to play a sport regularly. ......
  I love riding a bicycle. ......
  I think that the Internet helps bring people together. ......
- Write a reason for one of your answers.

  ----

go to Useful language p. 85

A Essay

Look at an example

1 Match the essay extracts 1–4 with sentences a–d below.

1

According to many scientists, one of the reasons we should eat meat is that if we don't, it is very difficult to maintain a healthy diet. A large number of important oils, acids and proteins that give us energy and strength and keep us healthy are found in meat and fish. If we lose balance in our diet, we can quickly get depressed and tired and suffer from memory problems.

However, vegetarians often claim that not eating meat is better for your health. They argue that...

2

Amateurs play a sport because they love it, whereas professionals see their sport as a career and aim to make as much money out of it as possible. Also, amateur sport is so much more part of the community than it is in professional sport, where players in teams are bought and sold not only from different regions but from different countries around the world.

3

There are lots of reasons why we should ride a bicycle more than we do. The first is that the environment is becoming seriously damaged by the amount of pollution caused by motor vehicles and if we used bicycles to make short journeys, we would reduce pollution enormously.

The second reason is …

4

What are the dangers of living in a world of virtual friendship?
One of the reasons that many normal, stable people nowadays look for a partner online is that they are not in a situation where they are able to meet new people; and if they do, there's often too little time to find out about the person's background and interests. It's not surprising then that internet dating has become so popular. Not only can we make contact with new people, but we can also decide whether we want to get to know them better before we actually meet them.
However, one of the consequences of the huge increase in online dating is that...

In this essay, the writer

a makes a comparison within each sentence. ..2..
b describes the cause of a situation in one paragraph and then starts to move on to its effect in another paragraph. ......

c gives some arguments 'for' in one paragraph and then starts to move on to arguments 'against'. ......
d seems to be trying to persuade the reader of one particular point of view. ......

2 Which title best fits each extract?

1
a 'Vegetarian diets are as healthy as diets containing meat.' Discuss.
b Don't eat meat! It's bad for you.

2
a 'Professional athletes don't deserve their money.' Do you agree?
b Compare and contrast the benefits of amateur and professional sports.

3
a 'Ride a bicycle – it's good for all of us!' Give your reasons.
b We must act now to prevent environmental disaster. Discuss.

4
a Finding a partner online. What are the advantages?
b Why is virtual friendship so popular and what are the dangers?

3 Answer these questions.

a In Extracts 1 and 3, why does the writer use a conditional (*if we don't… / if we used…*)? Write 1 and 3 in the gaps:
unlikely situation + result _____
possible situation + result _____

b In Extract 2, underline the uses of *their, they, it*. Who or what does each one refer to? [Example: *Amateurs play a sport because they love…* 'they' refers back to 'Amateurs'.]

c In Extract 4, underline the uses of *they, their, them*. Who does each one refer to?

Learning tip

We often use *they, them, their(s)* to avoid saying *he* or *she* after a singular noun or pronoun when we want to include people of either sex. However, even though the subject may be singular, we use a plural verb form: *We should give everyone an opportunity to say what **they** think.*

Focus on ...
avoiding repetition

Reference words are used to refer to people, objects and ideas that have been mentioned before or will be mentioned later. These words allow the writer to avoid repeating words and sometimes whole sentences. Examples: *it/they/them; him/his/her(s)/their(s); this/that/; these/those; one/ones; the former/the latter; (the) one/the other; such*

Change the words in brackets to avoid repetition.
a In some places meat-eating is on the decline. However, world-wide (*meat-eating*) __it__ is on the increase.
b Some professionals in sport are only interested in the money but (*the professionals who are only interested in the money*) _____ people tend not to last very long.
c There are at least two reasons why we should ride a bicycle. The first (*reason*) _____ is really common sense: it would help us reduce pollution.
d There's always a lot you want to know about another person: (*the other person's*) _____ interests, for example.
e There are many problems to overcome; one of (*the problems to overcome*) _____ is the security issue.
f Jack plays two sports, both football and rugby. He's quite good at (*football*) _____ but not so good at (*rugby*) _____ .

Plan

4 After a class discussion your English teacher has asked you to write an essay, giving your opinions on the following statement.

Working for yourself is better than working for someone else.

Answer the following questions.

a What will be the purpose of your essay? (e.g. to give a balanced view of two alternative points of view or to only argue one point of view.)

----

b Will you make comparisons within the same paragraph or present the arguments 'for' and 'against' in different paragraphs?

----

c What style will you use? (Think of who you are writing for.)

----

d What will make your reader think it is a good essay?

----

5 **Think of the advantages and disadvantages of working for yourself, and make notes.**

6 🔊**17** **Listen to a conversation between Ben and Samir and decide if there is anything you want to add to your notes.**

7 **Put your notes in order of importance. Which are the two most important advantages and disadvantages?**

8 **This is a possible paragraph plan for the essay.**

Paragraph 1: General introduction (whole picture/both sides of the argument)

Paragraph 2: Advantages
Advantage 1 → Reason and/or specific example
Advantage 2 → Reason and/or specific example

Paragraph 3: Disadvantages
Disadvantage 1 → Reason and/or specific example
Disadvantage 2 → Reason and/or specific example

Paragraph 4:
Summary/Balancing the argument
Giving your point of view

9 **Many paragraphs begin with a 'topic sentence' that makes it clear what the paragraph is going to be about. Match these topic sentences with the paragraphs above.**

a On the other hand, working for yourself gives you lots of worries. __Paragraph 3__
b Working for yourself has at least one main advantage. _____
c Many people today dream of being their own boss, but while working for yourself is an attractive prospect, the reality can sometimes be very different. _____
d On balance, though, working for yourself can give you a lot of job satisfaction. _____

10 **Look at the *Useful language* section on page 85 and select any phrases that would be useful to you.**

Write

11 **Write your essay in 200–250 words.**

Check

Now reread your essay and answer the following questions:

– Have you given your opinions on the statement: *Working for yourself is better than working for someone else*?
– Have you given both sides of the argument (*Working for yourself* AND *Working for someone else*)?
– Is each side of the argument in a separate paragraph?
– Is it clear by the end of the essay what your overall opinion is (for example, which of the two arguments you most agree with)?
– Is your style clear and neutral? (Remember, this is not a magazine article where you are often expected to be lively, provocative and amusing.)
– Have you used linking phrases to make the connections in your argument clear?
– Are the grammar, spelling, punctuation and your use of linking expressions accurate?

Make any changes that are necessary to your answer.

> **Learning tip**
>
> When writing an essay:
> ANALYZE
> Analyse the question and make sure you understand what you have to do. Think of:
> 1 the general topic
> 2 the specific aspect you have to write about
> 3 whether you are asked to describe, compare, give the arguments or persuade.
> BRAINSTORM
> Make notes of as many points as you can which answer the question.
> ORGANIZE
> Put your notes into a coherent shape (e.g. all the notes 'for' an argument and all the notes 'against'). Make sure they all answer the question.
> PLAN
> Prepare a paragraph plan. Think of a short introduction and a short conclusion.

E X tra practice

1 You have been asked by your teacher to write an essay comparing beach holidays with holidays in large cities. Make notes on:
  a The major differences between the two types of holiday.
  b Your preference, with reasons.

2 Organize your notes into an essay plan.
3 Think of a good opening sentence which focuses the attention of the reader.
4 Write your composition in about 200 words.

Class bonus

1 In pairs, brainstorm ideas on the following essay title: *In the twenty-first century we are too protective towards children. Do you agree?*
2 Organize your notes into paragraphs.
3 Draft your composition.
4 Move to your right and edit the other students' version. Consider:
  – paragraph construction
  – introduction and conclusion
  – sentence construction
  – linking expressions
  – vocabulary
  – spelling
  – punctuation
  – grammar (including verb forms)
  – word order.
  If you don't understand something, write *?*
5 Then move to your right once again and look at the edited version of an essay. Does it need editing further? Make improvements if necessary.

Can-do checklist

Tick what you can do.

	Can do	Need more practice
I can organize a paragraph plan for an essay.		
I can focus attention at the beginning of a paragraph.		
I can write clear, logical sentences.		
I can use reference words to avoid repetition.		
I can write a clearly argued and well-balanced essay.		

Unit 15
Facts and figures

Get ready to write

○ In your country, what do people spend more on? Choose one alternative:
food or rent? ....
gas/electricity/water or their telephone bills? ....
transport or leisure? ....
education or savings? ....
○ Which of these things do you spend most of your income on? ....

go to Useful language pp. 85–6

A Report based on charts, graphs and tables

Look at examples

1 Which of these is

a a *bar chart* comparing how much things have grown? ☐ 3
b a *pie chart* showing how a sum is divided? ☐
c a *table* comparing what people think? ☐

2 **STUDENT SATISFACTION SURVEY**

	VERY SATISFIED	SATISFIED	NOT SATISFIED
TEACHING	20%	65%	15%
STUDY FACILITIES	35%	45%	20%
MEALS	3%	27%	70%
LEISURE ACTIVITIES	62%	15%	23%
ACCOMMODATION	14%	35%	51%

Did you know ...?

– Britons spend more on takeaway meals than on fresh fruit and vegetables.
– Londoners appear to be the healthiest eaters: they spend nearly twice as much on fresh fruit and vegetables as those living in some other areas of the UK.

1 FAMILY SPENDING IN THE UK

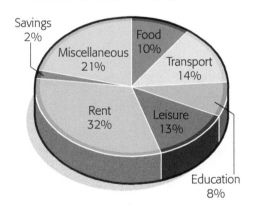

3

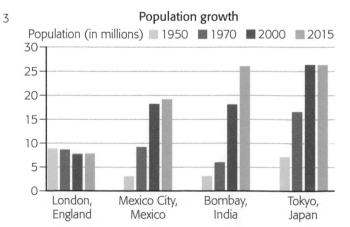

2 Match visuals 1–3 with these report extracts.

A ☑3

This chart shows changes in the population of London, Mexico City, Bombay and Tokyo from 1950 to a projected figure for 2015. In 1950 both Mexico City and Bombay had populations of under 5 million, but Mexico City's has since risen sharply to a projected figure of over 15 million; Bombay's increase has been even more dramatic, with a projected figure of over 25 million. While Tokyo had a sharp increase between 1950 (between 5 and 10 million) and 2000 (over 25 million), the figures since then have stayed constant. In the case of London, figures have remained fairly steady throughout the whole period at between 5 and 10 million, and indeed in recent years have dropped slightly.

B ☐

This table gives a clear picture of what the students like and don't like about the College. While most students (85%) are happy with the teaching, broadly happy with the study facilities (35% were very satisfied) and 62% very pleased with the leisure activities, over half are unhappy about the accommodation and 70% dissatisfied with the meals.

C ☐

This chart tells us about how the British spent their money last year.
As can be seen, the highest percentage was spent on rent (32%), followed by transport (14%) and leisure (13%). At the bottom end, only a small percentage was put aside as savings and a slightly larger amount spent on education. Both took just 10% of the total amount spent.

3 Answer these questions.

a How does each report begin?
A *This chart shows* _____
B _____
C _____

b In report A, what verb tense is mainly used? Why?
_____

c In report B, how do you know the students are still at the College? What tense would be used if they had left?
_____

d In report C, why is the passive used?
_____

e In all three reports not all the figures in the charts are mentioned. Why not?
_____

Focus on ...
analyzing trends

Trends are changes or movements. Situations stay the same (*remain stable, stay constant, keep at the same level*), they increase (*rise, grow*) or they decrease (*decline, collapse*).

There are a number of verbs (e.g. *expand, extend*) and nouns (e.g. *boom, growth*) to describe these movements. There are also many adjectives (e.g. *enormous, huge*) and adverbs (e.g. *gradually, considerably*) that go with them.

1 Look at this sales graph and <u>underline</u> the correct alternative below. 'This year' is 2008.

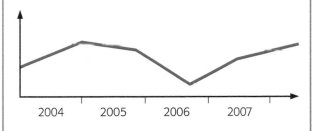

2004	2005	2006	2007

a In 2004 sales were <u>*up*</u> / *down*.
b In 2005 sales *fell dramatically / rose more steeply / fell slightly / stayed constant*.
c In 2006 there was a *steady improvement / slow decline / sharp drop* in sales.
d Last year there was a *significant improvement / steady decline*.
e This year the trend has been *upwards / downwards*.
f Sales *reached their peak / were at their lowest* in 2006.

2 Write the correct prepositions in the gaps.
a Compared __*with*__ last year, sales are up.
b With the exception _____ 2006, sales have been reasonable.
c There was a big increase _____ sales last year.
d _____ regard to this year, we are pleased to report good progress.

Plan

4 You have been asked by a geography teacher to write about the age structure of Canada for a college project. You have to describe the relative percentages (%) of the different age groups and the numbers of men and women in each. Look at the charts and answer the questions.

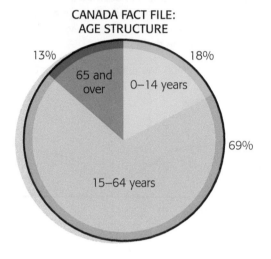

CANADA FACT FILE: AGE STRUCTURE

13% 65 and over
18% 0–14 years
69% 15–64 years

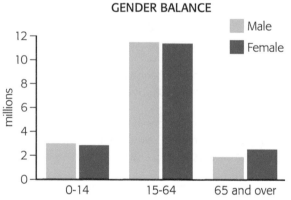

CANADA FACT FILE: GENDER BALANCE

Male / Female

millions (12, 10, 8, 6, 4, 2, 0)

0-14   15-64   65 and over

a Which is the largest and which is the smallest age group?
Largest: ....   Smallest: ....
b What else do you notice about the over-65 age group?
----
c What is the gender balance up to the age of 65?
----

5 Answer these questions.

a How many paragraphs will you have and what will each focus on?
b Is there any information you can combine?
c Which verb forms will you use?

Focus on ...
comparing information

When we compare information we use comparative forms (*greater than/more sharply than*), superlative forms (*the biggest increase/the most noticeable difference*) and (*not*) *as ... as* (*not as much was spent on ... as ...*). We also use modifiers such as *a great deal* (*more*), *far* (*less*), *easily* (*the largest*).

Correct the mistakes in these sentences.
a By far largest age group is the 15- to 64-year-olds.
By far the largest ....
b Much the most small group is the over-65s.
----
c There are significantly more women as men over 65.
----
d There are more or less the same number of boys than girls.
----
e These are the better statistics we have at present.
----
f They are meaningfuler that those in the previous survey.
----
g The more old the age group, the more great the gender difference.

Write

6 Write a draft of your report in about 100 words.

Check

Check your report. Tick ✓ which of these are true.

– I have included the information in Exercise 3 above. ☐
– I have only described the most significant information. ☐
– I have combined information where it would make my description clearer. ☐
– I have not repeated myself unnecessarily. ☐

Learning tip

When you talk about a chart or a table:
– say what its aim is and what it shows
– don't try and explain the reasons for data
– focus on the *main* information and trends – don't mention every detail
– make it clear what the figures in your description refer to
– avoid repetition.

E✗tra practice

1 🔊 **18** Jo has just attended a college lecture on changing social habits but didn't manage to copy down all the information. Look at the gaps in her chart. Can you guess what the missing figures will be? Listen to Jo talking to her colleague, Sophie, and check your guesses.

HOURS OF LEISURE TIME PER WEEK (AVERAGE PER HEAD)								
	10 YEARS AGO				THIS YEAR			
AGES	13–21	22–39	40–60	60+	13–21	22–39	40–60	60+
Watching TV	25	17	19	23	16	14	12	a
Playing on Computers	2	1	0.75	0.5	14	b	3.5	4
Cinema	1.25	2	1.5	2.25	c	1	0.75	2
Sport/exercise	7	4.5	4	4.75	4	1.5	d	5.5
Socializing	10	8.75	6.5	2.5	3.5	5.25	2.5	e

2 Use this table to write a report comparing the time spent on leisure activities ten years ago with now. Describe only the most important differences. There are clues in the conversation between Jo and Sophie to help you.

3 Edit your answer.
   – Check you have mentioned all five categories and only described the most important difference in each.
   – If you have used these expressions, check you have used the correct preposition:
   compared with, with the exception of, a big increase in, more time is spent on, in/with regard to

Class bonus

1 You are going to do a survey on what people eat. Find out about the people in your class using the following questions.
   a Do you eat at least three pieces of fruit a day?
   b Do you eat meat every day?
   c Do you eat fish at least twice a week?
   d Is more than 20% of your diet 'junk food'?
   e Do you eat fresh vegetables every day?
   f Do you eat between meals?

2 Complete this graph to show the number of students who answered 'yes' to each question.

3 Write a report summarizing your findings.
4 Compare your reports.

Can-do checklist

Tick what you can do.

	Can do	Need more practice
I can interpret information for a report.		
I can describe graphs, charts and tables.		
I can select and summarize the most important information.		
I can describe information in a logical order.		
I can write a report describing information in charts.		

Unit 16
Short and to the point

Get ready to write

○ Some organizations ask public relations companies to summarize relevant articles from the media for them.
  a Why do you think summaries are useful for busy people? b What do you think a summary should include?

go to Useful language p. 86

A Summary of an article

Look at an example

**1 Read the article below and <u>underline</u> the key points.
Which paragraphs contain most of these points?**

Club Med goes to MOROCCO

1 The things we do to relax! Here I am trying not to scream as a powerful Moroccan masseuse attacks every tense muscle in my body. I am at the Cinq Mondes spa in Marrakesh, where you can have traditional Moroccan massages and body scrubs or relax in the Turkish bath rooms.

2 Cinq Mondes is part of Club Med's new La Palmeraie resort, an attempt by the French holiday resort company to make its image more exclusive. The idea is that Club Med (short for *Club Méditerranée*) must change to cater for its customers' changing tastes. The traditional Club Med customer has become older and wealthier, and now expects a certain degree of luxury.

3 First established as a not-for-profit association in 1950, Club Med started as an idealistic village on the Spanish island of Majorca with members staying in unlit straw huts on a beachfront, sharing washing facilities. Over time, the number of villages increased greatly in exotic locations around the world, and eventually the villages were replaced with modern blocks or huts with en suite facilities. Originally attracting singles and young couples, the Club later became primarily a destination for families, although the concept of membership was retained, with each customer paying a joining and annual membership fee. Unfortunately, the strategy was not successful. The company made such huge losses that in 2002 a new strategy was announced: they would concentrate once more on the idea of holiday villages but for wealthy holidaymakers.

4 The original idea behind Club Med was that each resort would provide an extensive list of services and activities in one single package, with the emphasis on friendliness and multiculturalism. Club Med staff were called GOs (*gentils organisateurs*) and its clients called GMs (*gentils membres*), and GOs and GMs would play, dine, drink and dance together every night. Now though the emphasis is on choice, so that Club Meds offer different dining experiences, different levels of accommodation and different levels of pricing. Offers are being aimed at families, those seeking indulgence in the latest spa treatments, independent travellers looking for a quiet time, and the classic club mix of 24-hour party people wanting action, adventure, dancing and fun.

5 So here I am in La Palmeraie, a wonderful place to be if you're looking for a quiet oasis after the bustle of Marrakesh. Having completed my treatments, I have taken my place by the poolside next to the perfectly polished French ladies and am feeling very pleased with myself.

2 This is a summary of about 120 words written for the editor of a holiday guide book. Which of the key points that you underlined are in the summary?

a Which paragraphs in the original article provide most of the information?

b Why are the first and last paragraphs not used?

c What information does the summary include that you have not underlined (if anything)?

3 What extra information would you include in a summary of 200 words?

According to the article, Club Med has had to develop a more exclusive image and offer more choice to its customers.

Originally, when Club Med opened in 1950, it was 'an idealistic village … with members staying in unlit straw huts on a beachfront, sharing washing facilities'. Staff and clients would 'play, dine, drink and dance together every night'. Later, its market moved from singles and young couples to families, and the company abandoned the idea of the village while keeping the principle of club membership. However, the approach was commercially unsuccessful and in 2002 the company decided to return to 'the idea of holiday villages but for wealthy holidaymakers'.

Now, Club Med is offering different experiences for different types of clients at different prices.

Focus on …
quotations

Direct quotations from the original article can sometimes bring a summary to life. However, they normally help the summary develop and do not normally simply illustrate points already made. Look at the examples of how to include quotations.

1 …*the company decided to return to 'the idea of holiday villages but for wealthy holidaymakers'.*
As the quotation is part of the sentence and its meaning, there is no comma or colon before the first quotation mark.

2 *According to the writer, 'Unfortunately, the strategy was not successful.'*
Here, to introduce the quotation, the phrase *According to the writer* is followed by a comma.

3 *A different strategy was needed: 'Now … the emphasis is on choice.'*
Here, a colon is used to introduce a quoted phrase. Also, three dots are used to show that you have cut one or more words from the original article.

Notice that in the second and third examples the final full stop comes inside the quotation marks.

Correct the punctuation mistakes in these sentences.
a Later it became, 'primarily a destination for families'.
b It is 'an attempt … to make its image more exclusive".
c Customers expect 'a certain degree of luxury'
d It was different in 1950; 'Club Med started as an idealistic village'.
e As the article says 'each resort would provide .... services and activities in one single package'.

Plan

4 You have been asked to find interesting articles on changes and developments in UK restaurants and make summaries where appropriate.

Read through the newspaper article on page 76 quickly. <u>Underline</u> the main points that answer these questions.

a What tradition is disappearing from Greek restaurants in the UK?
b Why is it disappearing?
c What has it been replaced with in some restaurants?
d How has the tradition been interpreted?
e Will some restaurateurs continue the tradition?

5 Make notes on the most important points you will include in your summary (Note: examples of how the tradition has been interpreted might make the summary interesting). Do not add your own opinion or interpretation.

6 Put the notes in logical order.

7 Write an opening sentence to introduce and summarize the overall situation. (You do not need to write a concluding sentence.)

Did you know …?

Almost every Jewish wedding ends with the bridegroom breaking a glass with his foot. One interpretation is that it is a reminder of how fragile personal relationships can be and that the bride and groom should take care.

SMASHING GREEK CUSTOM GOES TO THE WALL

Fearing they will be sued by diners hit by flying crockery, hundreds of owners of Greek restaurants in the UK are no longer allowing their customers to smash plates.

"Smashing plates in restaurants is a nice Greek tradition but what can you do?" said Chris Toumaz, who runs Trios in Palmers Green, north London. "All these claims now, everyone's just looking for an excuse to sue you. We have stopped doing it."

Some restaurateurs have replaced plates with less dramatic alternatives. "We're throwing flowers now," said Nikos Constantinou, the manager of the Apollo Restaurant Taverna, in Islington, north London. "It's not as messy and if you hit someone it doesn't really matter."

Mr Constantinou, 30, said he called a halt to the custom about two years ago after a woman customer was hit in the face by a flying fragment of crockery and had to go to hospital for stitches for a cut above her eyebrow. "She didn't sue, but we were worried someone would," he said.

Over the centuries, breaking plates has become linked to the Greek concept of *kefi* (high spirits and fun). Some say that it keeps away evil spirits. Others maintain that plates broken during a wedding reception symbolize good luck and a happy, lasting marriage.

Expressing his own theory of why the tradition started, Mr Constantinou said: "It relieves your worries. If you are stressed or upset you can release it all by breaking the plates. I suppose it can also be done to show appreciation for the music or the dancing. Over the years it has been interpreted in different ways."

The restaurateurs all agreed that the plates used for smashing should be cheap ones that crumble harmlessly. In the wrong hands, however, even these can be harmful. Fights have been known to start after fragments of crockery landed in another customer's moussaka.

"We are worried that they will start smashing the good plates which cost £5 each," said one owner. He put up a sign telling customers to leave all plate smashing to trained staff.

Some Greek restaurateurs, however, insist that they will continue the tradition. Stefano Floridas, of Athens Restaurant in Eastbourne, East Sussex, said that the town's Greek community would continue smashing plates at family parties held every three months. "It's a tradition that's been going on for hundreds of years," he said. "It's ridiculous that they've stopped doing it."

Focus on ...
sentence combining

A compound sentence is when two separate sentences are joined by a connecting expression like *and, and then, but, neither/nor* etc.
Plate smashing can be great fun. It can be dangerous.
Plate smashing can be great fun **but** *(it) can be dangerous.*

A 'complex sentence' is when there are parts of a sentence that are dependent on other parts of a sentence. They cannot be written as separate sentences.
***When/If you smash a plate**, (dependent part) // you need to be careful. (main part)*
***To be on the safe side**, // some restaurants are using flowers instead of plates.*

Complete these sentences in two different ways to make one compound or complex sentence. Make any changes necessary to the sentence to make it sound natural.

a Restaurant owners fear they will be sued by customers. The tradition of smashing plates is disappearing.
The tradition of smashing plates is disappearing because restaurant owners fear they will be sued by customers.
Fearing they will be sued by customers, owners say the tradition of smashing plates is disappearing.

b It is less dangerous to throw flowers than plates. Some restaurateurs have replaced plates with flowers.
To make it ....
Since ....

c There are many risks. Some restaurateurs still allow plate smashing.
Despite ....
.... but ....

d Some restaurateurs will still allow plate smashing. They want to continue the tradition.
Wanting ....
.... because ....

Write

8 Rewrite your notes as a summary of about 100 words. Use your own words as far as possible.

Check

Check your summary and make any necessary changes.

- Will the editor understand the summary and find it interesting?
- Does your opening sentence give some idea of the paragraph as a whole?
- Have you included the most important points?
- Have you included some examples?
- Is the summary clear and concise? Have you left out any unnecessary repetition?
- If you had to reduce it further, what would you exclude?
- Have you included any compound and/or complex sentences?
- Are your spelling and punctuation correct?

Class bonus

1 Read the article on page 15.
2 Who can create the shortest summary that includes all the necessary information?

E✗tra practice

1 🔊 **19** Your company does business in Japan and is preparing some advice on business etiquette. Your manager has asked you to listen to a podcast and make a summary of the main points. Listen to the podcast and make notes.

2 Write an email summary of the podcast in about 140 words. You may use this outline to help you.

Japanese business etiquette is quite different ....
....

Appearance
Both ....
Business entertaining
....
However, an invitation to ....
....

Gift-giving
It is customary to ....
Business cards
....

Physical gestures
Another point to remember is ....
....
However, despite these 'rules', ...
....

---

3 Now look again at your summary. Are there any words or phrases that could be cut without losing the main meaning? Are there any important points missing? Make any changes that are necessary.

Can-do checklist

Tick what you can do.

	Can do	Need more practice
I can skim an article and identify key points.		
I can sequence the points in logical order for a summary.		
I can rewrite and summarize key points in my own words.		
I can use quotations, where appropriate, with correct punctuation.		
I can write compound and complex sentences.		

A Abbreviating

How could you shorten these when making notes?

a frequently ...freq...
b that is to say ....
c kilometres per hour ....

d department ....
e number ....
f good ....

g compare ....
h therefore ....
i for example ....

j the same as ....
k and so on ....
l Managing Director ....

B Summarizing

Reduce this extract from a newspaper article to about 40 words by completing the gaps in the summary.

MONEY CAN'T BUY HAPPINESS

The Beatles told us that money can't buy love, but it takes an economist to tell us that it can't buy happiness. A new index of well-being shows that the world's wealthiest countries do very badly when it comes to true contentment.

The index attempts to measure how well countries use their resources to deliver longer lives, greater physical well-being and satisfaction. It finds that true happiness can be had on the Pacific island of Vanuatu which comes out as number one.

By contrast the Group of Eight (G8) rich nations, whose leaders gather for their annual summit in St Petersburg this weekend, languish near the bottom of the list.

Some research published this week shows that you don't

.... (maximum 7 words). On the

list of the world's .... (maximum

2 words) the richest countries ....

(maximum 4 words) and the tiny Pacific island of Vanuatu

.... (maximum 2 words).

C Writing a letter of complaint

This is a semi-formal letter of complaint. <u>Underline</u> the best alternative.

I am writing to (a) *tell you / <u>complain</u>* about the poor level of service (b) *you've given to me / provided by your company*.

Two months ago I signed up for a deal for cable TV, cable internet and telephone, but since then (c) *I have had nothing but problems / you've made my life very difficult*.

(d) *Right, first / First of all* the initial installation was cancelled, resulting in me waiting a whole day for (e) *your technician to arrive / one of your guys to turn up*. Then when he didn't arrive, I spent ages on your (f) *uncooperative / very unhelpful* telephone support line, with a mechanical voice telling me to check your website, which was impossible since I had no web access.

(g) *Eventually, / At last* the installation was rescheduled for two weeks later but when the technician arrived he didn't have the necessary tools to do the job. (h) *However / On top of that*, two weeks and many mobile phone calls later, my modem still hasn't arrived, even though I have begun to pay for internet access. (i) *Overall, / Furthermore*, I am still waiting for my telephone connection.

It goes without saying that I am extremely (j) *fed up / dissatisfied* and wish to cancel my contract with immediate effect.

D Writing instructions

🔊 **20** Listen to someone describing how to cook Venetian rice and bean soup. Make notes and write a set of simple instructions for a recipe book.

VENETIAN RICE AND BEAN SOUP

Ingredients

300 g ....
.... beans
½ l ....
.... (chopped)
.... butter
.... bacon (diced)
.... olive oil
Salt and ....

1 .... the beans and .... , then ....
2 .... the oil and butter in .... and ....
3 After a few minutes, ... , cover .... and ....
4 .... and .... on a moderate heat ....
5 .... stock and ....
6 ....

E Writing up notes

These are some notes taken during a Climate Change Conference.
Write them up as a permanent record.

CLIMATE CHANGE CONFERENCE
November 16th
10.30 Guy Richard's opening lecture
Recent devels. Main concs: greenhouse gases →
climate change; global temps. likely to ↑ 1.4 –
5.8°C this cent.; risks more serious than prev.
thought.

Guy Richard's Plenary on ....
opened the conference and his main conclusions
were that
1 climate change ....
2 global temperatures ....
3 ....

F Making an itinerary

🔊 **21** Listen to a travel agent giving you some
details of the first part of your holiday and
complete this itinerary.

MULTI-ACTIVITY HOLIDAY IN SOUTH AFRICA

ITINERARY (Draft)

Monday:
Tuesday:
Wednesday:
Thursday:
Friday:

G Reporting

This is part of a report about current shopping
habits in a town. Complete the sentences with
words and phrases from the box.

That will be
£121.45

significant	gave out questionnaires	interviewed
majority of	included	convenience
disappointed	although	purchases
savings		

The vast (a) ...._majority of_........ shoppers questioned said
they still used shops in the town centre but a
(b) .... percentage (40%) said they had
also made (c) .... on the Internet in the
last three months. The reasons they gave
(d) .... :

1 (e) .... : it was easier to shop online
 than to shop in town
2 cost: they were able to make (f) ....
 by shopping online, (g) .... some said
 they had been (h) .... by high shipping
 costs.

H Writing accurately

Correct the mistakes in this extract from a student's composition.

To live (a ......*Living*......) in another country is a really intresting
(b ....) experience but it can have very important affects
(c ....) on ones (d ....) life.

The worse (e ....) thing that, (f ....) most people finds
(g ....) is that they miss there (h ....) family and all the
facilites (i ....) that they use (j ....) have
(k ....) back home. It's only then that they start to apreciate
(l ....) everything they had.

Second (m ....) you soon realize that you have to be responsable
(n...........................) for everything you do if you will want (o ....)
to acheive (p ....) your goals. Nobody else are going to clean
(q ....) your room or wash your cloths (r ....)
– only you.

I Sentence construction

Combine the sentences using the word(s) in brackets.

a   Theo carried on working. He wasn't feeling well. (*despite*)
    Despite not feeling well, Theo carried on working........................

b   I've applied for a job with an export company. I know nothing about it. (*about which*)
    ----

c   I hadn't eaten for 24 hours. I felt very hungry. (*Not having*)
    ----

d   I'm going to write to your parents. You haven't been to class for the last two weeks! (*Since*)
    ----

e   I'll post the letter today. I want to make sure it gets there for your brother's birthday. (*to*)
    ----

f   We decided to take the flat. We knew we couldn't afford the rent. (*While knowing*)
    ----

g   I entered the room. I realized something was wrong. (*After*)
    ----

h   I was attacked by Tania's dog. I didn't want to go round to her house again. (*Having*)
    ----

i   Marco wore a raincoat. He didn't want to get wet. (*so that*)
    ----

j   You saw your old friend. What was your reaction? (*on*)

J Reflecting

a   What are the most important things you learnt in Units 7–16?
    ----

b   Which units/sections did you find the most useful?
    ----

c   Which of your writing skills have you improved most since starting this book?
    ----

d   Which writing tasks do you still need more practice in?

Appendix 1
Useful language

This section contains a list of words, combinations of words, phrases and abbreviations that might be useful to you in completing the task in the unit or a similar task. You can use the list in different ways.

1 You can look at the list before you begin the unit and make sure you understand the meaning of the words and phrases by looking them up in a dictionary. Abbreviations which come up in the unit are explained and looking at these will make the unit easier for you.

2 You can refer to the list before you write your first draft of the writing task or have it by your side as you are writing.

3 You can look at the list when you have completed the unit and check you understand the words and phrases. You might want to make a separate record in a vocabulary book of any you find particularly useful.

When you start using the book, you may prefer to use the list in the first way. However, in most units, the list will be useful when you come to write your draft. Since many of the units contain different ways of beginning a sentence, you might want to try to complete the sentences and decide which sentence fits your draft best.

Unit 1

1 Formal
Could you **inform** me (whether) … ?
I'm **uncertain** (when) …
Would it be acceptable if (we) …

Informal
Could you **tell** me (whether) … ?
I'm **not sure** (when) …
Is it OK if (we) …

2 Saying why you're writing
I saw your advertisement in … and I …
I'm writing to you because …
The reason I'm writing is that …

3 Referring to an advertisement
In your advertisement you say that …
(but I) …
You don't say exactly …

4 Introducing a request in writing
I'm very interested in … but I would like to …
We'll (probably) be arriving on … so …
Since we'll be arriving on … (could we/could you) …
While we're there we … (not only want to … but we'd like to …)

5 Asking for information
Could you tell me if/whether …?
I would like to know if/whether …
Do you have any …?
Could you give me (some idea/precise details) …?
I need to know a bit about …
Is there an extra charge for …?
My final question is …

6 Accommodation vocabulary
rent (an apartment/a room)
book/make a booking (at a b&b)
central heating
air conditioning

7 Abbreviations
v.imp. (very important)
p.w. (per week)
b&b (bed and breakfast – room and early morning meal in a private house or small hotel)
TV (television)

Unit 2

1 Giving polite thanks
We want to give special thanks/our most grateful thanks to …
It was very/so kind of you to …
I sincerely hope I can repay you …

2 Friendly thanks
Thank you/Thanks so much for …
I'm writing to thank you for …

3 Offering sympathy
I'm really sorry to hear that …
I was very sad to hear about …
I know how much …
I hope this doesn't mean that …
Please accept my deepest sympathy.

4 Giving congratulations
Formal: On behalf of …, I would like to congratulate you on …
Informal: I'm very glad to hear that …
We've just heard the news.
Congratulations! We're all delighted.

5 Common abbreviations in letters
Cc (carbon copy – when you send a copy of a letter to more than one person)
Re: (with reference to – concerning)
Enc: (enclosure – when you include other papers with your letter)
pp (*per procurationem* – a Latin phrase meaning that you are signing the letter because the writer is not there to sign it)
PS (post script – when you want to add something extra at the end of a letter after you have signed it. Not usually used in business and formal letters)

6 Letter/email openings
If you know the person's name:
Dear Mr/Ms + family name (*Miss* and *Mrs* are usually only used if you know the person)
If you don't know the person's name:
Dear Sir or Madam or *Dear Sir/Madam*
Dear Sirs is sometimes used but is thought to be sexist.
Dear Human Resources Manager
Informal
Dear + given name (*Tom*)

7 Letter/email closings
Business and formal
Yours sincerely (if you know the person's name)
Yours faithfully (usually only when you don't know the person's name)
Informal
Best wishes
Kind regards

Unit 3

1 Short phrases for noticeboards
Loves Italian food.
No smokers, please.
Brand-new fridge.
Perfect condition.
Spare ticket available.
Anyone interested?
Lift wanted.

2 Abbreviations
km (kilometres)
vgc (very good condition)
mins (minutes)
inc. (included/including)
no. (number)
3-wk (three-week)
pref. (preferably)
nr. (near)
postgrad. (postgraduate)

3 Participles
Past participles
Bike stolen
Cat found
Lost iPod
Accommodation offered
A young woman recently graduated …

Present participles
Looking for a new partner.
Hoping to exchange old Peugeot
Not enjoying college life
A young woman graduating this year …

Unit 4

Forms
Names
Title
First name
Middle initial(s)
Surname
Maiden name

Personal details
Date of birth
Gender
Marital status (single, married, divorced, separated, living with partner)
Number of dependent children
First language
Occupation
Passport No.

Address
Correspondence address (permanent/temporary)
County
Country
Postcode
Email address

Payment details
Amount to be sent
credit/debit card
expiry date

Identification
Signature

Instructions
Please tick here (✓)/Please mark with a X
Write not applicable (N/A) where appropriate
* Items with asterisks must be completed
Complete in BLOCK CAPITALS only.
State clearly in the box the date you want…

Unit 5

1 Giving the context
I'm writing this from …
Well, here I am in …
It seems hard to believe I've been here in … for …

2 Describing a place
This place is …
There is/There are …
The thing I really like about this place is …
One thing I'm not very keen on is …

3 Adjective word order
opinion + size + age + shape + colour
a   lovely   old
+ material + nationality + noun
   stone   house

4 Pairs of adjectives
*This place is very **interesting**.*
(to describe the place) / *I'm very **interested** in this place.* (to describe its effect on you)
boring/bored; fascinating/fascinated; tiring/tired; frightening/frightened; exciting/excited

5 Adverb + adjectives
– To make adjectives stronger:
  *The palace is **very**/**extremely**/**remarkably** beautiful.*
– To make adjectives weaker: *The hotel was **rather**/**fairly**/**pretty**/**a bit**/**a little**/**quite** small.*
– To emphasize ungradable (extreme) adjectives: *It was **absolutely freezing**.* (Not ~~very freezing~~)

6 adverb + adjective combinations
bitterly cold; perfectly safe; seriously damaged; totally inadequate; utterly impossible; heavily polluted

Unit 6

1 Evaluative adjectives
Positive
outstanding, entertaining, impressive, moving, memorable, stylish, sensitive, imaginative, lovely, lifelike, passionate, romantic

Negative
disappointing, tedious, weak, predictable, depressing

2 Adjective + noun combinations
compulsive viewing, gripping thriller, action-packed war film, hilarious comedy, loud applause, a very different type of (…), no real plot

3 Adverb + adjective combinations
Positive
(pretty) good, (surprisingly) effective, (highly) watchable, (deeply) inspiring, (incredibly) thought-provoking, (particularly) interesting, (totally) convincing, (hugely) successful, (highly) amusing, (truly) original, (really) lively, (extremely) popular, (quite) sophisticated

Negative
(a bit) flat, (rather) woolly/vague, (disappointingly) brief, (utterly) ridiculous, not very well-made/well-written/well-directed/well-produced (movie)

4 Describing and giving opinions about the content
(This) is a story about …
It is set in …
The character(s) I like most are …
(it) is based on …
(X) argues (quite/very) strongly that …
The best part is when …
I like/don't like the beginning/ending because …

5 Recommending/Not recommending

Get there early.
Great family entertainment
My only grumble is that …

6 Summarizing

All in all, (it) …
Quite simply, (this is) …

Unit 7

1 Acronyms

asap (as soon as possible)
aka (also known as)
a.m. (*ante meridiem*: after midnight and before midday)
p.m. (*post meridiem*: after midday and before midnight)
BTW (by the way)
FYI (for your information)
TBA (to be announced)
VIP (very important person)
IT (information technology)

2 Abbreviations

e.g. (for example)
etc. (and so on)
c.f. (compare)
i.e. (that is to say)
no. (number)
kph (kilometres per hour)
mph (miles per hour)

3 Common shortenings

est. (estimated)
pref. (preferably)
v. (very)
intro. (introduction)
?s (questions)
p.t. (part time)
f.t. (full time)
freq. (frequently)
pop. (popular)
avail. (available)
dpt. (department)
cont. or *cont'd* or *cont/d* (continued)
reps (representatives)
ltd (limited)
wks (weeks)
dif. (different)
admin. (administration)

4 Symbols

(60)+ (over/more than)
= (the same as)
∴ (therefore)
∵ (because)
>> (much more than)
→ (which leads to)
✓ (good) ✓✓ (very good)

Unit 8

1 Telling someone what to do

(You) turn (left at …)
(You) get off (the bus at …)
You'll need to/I suggest you (buy some extra milk).

2 Giving reasons/Stating purpose

To (get to the Underground you …)
In order to (open a bank account you have to …)

3 Words and phrases to show sequence

First(ly), Second(ly), Third(ly) … , etc.
Next …/Then …/After this (that) … /
Following this (that) …/Now (you) …/
At this point …/… and then …
Lastly/Finally …
When (the person answers you …) …/
On (discovering a fire) you …
If you (hear the alarm, you …)
Before (entering) …

4 Saying how you do something

(Get the pilot light lit) by … (press)ing …

5 Giving strong instructions

You should/shouldn't (enter your PIN number).

Unit 9

1 Before the meeting

call/hold/plan/have a meeting
invite someone to attend a meeting
draw up/circulate an agenda
items on the agenda

2 At the meeting

chair/lead the meeting
Apologies for absence: (+ NAMES)
Participants: (+ NAMES)
in the chair/the chairperson
keep/take minutes
brainstorm ideas
ask for contributions from …

discuss/deal with/consider an issue (at length/in detail/in depth)
make a point/a proposal/a suggestion
give your view
raise an issue
reach an agreement/a compromise/a decision
bring matters to a conclusion
make a proposal/recommendation
take a decision/a vote
bring the meeting to a close/close the meeting
adjourn the meeting until …

3 After the meeting

write a report
write up/circulate the minutes

4 Seminars

an all-day/a one-day seminar
give/conduct/attend a seminar on …

Unit 10

1 Complaints

Formal openings
I'm writing on account of/to express my extreme concern that …
I'm afraid I'm forced to write to you to object to/to draw your attention to/to complain about …

Explaining the problem
I appreciate the reasons for … but …
The problems did not stop there.
In addition, (I would like to remind you) …/Even worse …/Even more worrying…

Giving your opinion/feelings
I find it very disappointing that …
You do not seem to realize that …
I'm very surprised (that such a reputable organization) …

Saying what you hope and want to happen
I trust that the situation does not …
I would appreciate it if you would …
I would be grateful if you could …
I demand that you …
I would urge you to …
I (would) hope that in future …
I must insist that you …
I feel something ought to be done.
It's time you …
Please can you assure me that …

Saying what you will do
If I do not get a satisfactory response I will have no alternative but to …
I will take further action if …

Informal

This strikes me as (ridiculous).

What's more/On top of that …

2 Apologies

Formal

I apologize most sincerely for …

I must apologize for …

I'd like to apologize for (not) … +-*ing*

Informal

I'm really very sorry (that I … /to have done/not to have done) …

Unit 11

1 Requests

Informal

Can you …/Could you …?

Do you think you could …?

Polite

Would you mind …?

I wonder if you'd mind …

I'd be very grateful if you could …?

Would it be possible (for you) to …?

I was wondering whether you could …/whether it would be possible if you could …

Would you be so kind as to …?

2 Offers

Informal

Shall I …?

I'll …

Polite

Would you like me to …?

If you'd like me to … I could …/I would be (quite) happy to …

3 Accepting politely

Thank you for offering to …

I'd be very happy/pleased/delighted to accept.

4 Refusing

Informal

Sorry about not being able to … but …

Polite

Thank you for … but unfortunately, I can't …/it's not possible for me to …

Sorry about not being able to … but …

I'm terribly sorry … but I can't … I didn't realize …

I'm afraid I am unable to …/I will not be able to …

It was very kind of you to … but …

Unit 12

1 Writing reports

Introduction

The aim/purpose of this report is to …

The main aims are to …

This report describes/outlines …

Carrying out research

I have discussed the issue with …

Most (employees) interviewed seem …

The (vast) majority of (those interviewed) thought/felt/agreed that …

About … per cent of … said that …

Very few (of) … believed that …

A small but significant minority (of) …

According to …

Making generalizations

On balance, …/All things considered …

Broadly speaking …

(It seems/appears that) on the whole, …/in the main …

Generally, …/It was generally felt that …

In short …

Conclusion

In conclusion, …

Our survey suggests/showed that …

In my view/the view of (most people interviewed), we (should) …

Based on this research/information, we (have no hesitation in recommending) …

2 Adverbs suggesting the writer's attitude

(un)fortunately, presumably, in theory, ideally, evidently, apparently, admittedly, obviously, strictly speaking, (not) surprisingly, clearly

Unit 13

Comparing and contrasting

While/Whereas X is … Y is …

Neither …/Both …

Although …/Even though …

In spite of …/Despite …

In spite of …/Despite the fact that …

However …

Instead, …

Conversely, …

In comparison …

On the contrary, …

By (way of) contrast …

Unit 14

1 Balancing arguments

On the one hand … on the other hand …

While it is true that …, it has to be said that …

2 Reporting on views

According to …

Many people think/claim that …

However, people often argue that …

It is often said that …

3 Introducing a topic

Why do some people believe that …?

First of all I'd like to say that …

The first point I'd like to make is …

I'd like to begin by …

In the first place …/Firstly, … it is important to remember that …

To begin with …

In addition, /What is more, /Furthermore, …

Another advantage is …

Then, there is …

Finally …/ Last but not least, …

4 Introducing an opinion

In my opinion, …

It is clear/obvious that …

I think/believe that …

There is no doubt that …

It is well known that …

5 Giving reasons

One of the many reasons that/for …

There are lots of reasons …

6 Giving advantages and disadvantages

The main advantage …

One big disadvantage …

7 Summarizing

In conclusion, …

On balance, I feel that …

To sum up …/However, in my view/from my point of view …)

Unit 15

1 Charts, graphs, tables

Pie chart: segment

Chart/table: row, column

Graph (bar graph, line graph): solid line, dotted line, broken line

2 Describing patterns

This (chart) shows that/represents …
It gives (the number of hours) …
As can be seen from (the chart) …
According to (Table 1) …
Looking at the (figures) in …
It is estimated that …
As far as (X) are concerned …

3 Analyzing trends

Verbs

increase, climb, shoot up, leap, rocket, soar
stabilize, level off, fluctuate
decrease, decline, slump, plummet, dive

Sales were up/down/at their lowest/at
their highest (level)
are continuing to rise/fall
went up/rose/improved (slightly/
steadily/dramatically/sharply/
steeply)
went down/fell (noticeably/
markedly/gradually)
recovered/got better/got worse
(moderately/rapidly)
levelled off/stabilized/stayed the
same/remained stable
reached a (their) peak/a maximum
reached a low point/hit rock
bottom
fluctuated

There has been
a dramatic/sudden increase in
(a) steady/significant improvement in
(a) moderate growth in
a levelling off of
a slow/slight decline in
a sharp drop in

There has been an upward/downward
trend. / The trend has been upwards/
downwards.

4 Comparisons

there are more/less/fewer … than …
(prices) fell more sharply/steeply in …
than …
by far the largest …
twice the number/twice as many
(approximately/roughly/nearly/about)
three times as many
(just over/under) a half/double the
number (of) … in comparison with/as
opposed to …
in contrast …
…, respectively
… in particular

Unit 16

1 Compound sentences

Club Med staff were called GOs *and/and
then* its clients (were) called GMs.
Club Med staff were called GOs – its
clients were called GMs. (informal)
Its market moved to families *but/yet* the
approach was unsuccessful.

2 Complex sentences

Noun clauses

What they decided to do was replace
plates with flowers.
The owners fear (that) they will be sued.
Whether or not the tradition will die out,
nobody knows.
*Worried the customers would start
smashing good plates*, the owners put up
notices (telling them not to do it).

Relative clauses

The owners put up notices *which told
them/telling them not to do it*.

Adverbial clauses

When/If you receive a business card,
treat it respectfully.
*Although foreigners make many
mistakes in etiquette*, the Japanese are
very understanding.
Business people dress conservatively
because they want to be taken seriously.

Appendix 2
Punctuation

1 Full stop ('period' in American English)

– to show the end of the sentence: *She went out.*
– in abbreviations: *p. etc.*
– for decimals (*1.5%*), units of time (*6.30*) and units of money (*£6.80*)
– for email/website addresses: *www.cambridge.org/elt*
However, with some abbreviations, full stops are a matter of style and are sometimes omitted (*the USA, Mr Dylan*).

2 Capital letter

– to begin a sentence: *We were late.*
– for the pronoun *I*, names, titles, countries, nationalities, streets, cities, days of the week and months (not seasons) of the year: *Tom and I went to Paris on the first Saturday in June.*
– for the main words in titles of books, films, songs and magazines: *The Last King of Scotland*, *War and Peace*

3 Question mark

– at the end of a direct question: *What time is it?*

4 Exclamation mark

– to express emotional emphasis in informal writing: *What a lovely place!*

5 Apostrophe

– to show there is a missing letter (a contraction): *It's mine.* (= *It is*)
– to show possession: *My brother's house.* (one brother) *My brothers' house.* (more than one brother)

6 Comma

In general terms, we can use a comma to divide a sentence into sections to make it easier to understand. The rules are not always very exact. However, we usually use a comma:
– to link two statements when there is a different subject in each part (*It was a lovely day, but I decided not to go out.*)
– when a sentence has a linking word like *when* or *although*. (*Although it rained a lot, we enjoyed our holiday.*)
– to separate items in a list: *a comb, brush(,) and shaving cream.* (The use of a comma before *and* is more common in American English.)

– to separate an introductory word or phrase: *Unfortunately, we …*
– to separate a question tag: *He plays the piano well, doesn't he?*
– around inserted phrases and clauses: *Rio, which is on the coast, is …* (non-defining relative clause); *I did, however, manage to …*; *It is, as you know, a …*
– in direct speech: *'I'm going,' he said. He said, 'I'm going.'*

7 Colon

– to introduce a list (*There wasn't much in the cupboard: a pair of shoes, a jacket, an old shirt …*)
– in more formal writing to add extra information, an explanation, a quotation or an example: *There are two cafés: Starbucks and the …*

8 Semi-colon

– to separate two main clauses that have a link in meaning: *The clouds were heavy; it was raining …* Note: we could also use a full stop here but a full stop suggests a bigger break in meaning.

9 Dash

A dash is often used in informal writing:
– instead of a colon or semi-colon
– to separate a statement that is extra to the main idea: *We went to Peru – in fact most of the time we spent in Cuzco. The old lady – Mrs Jones – was very upset she had lost her dog.* (In the second example, the dashes are like brackets: *The old lady (Mrs Jones) was…*)

10 Quotation/speech marks

– to separate direct speech from the rest of the sentence: *'You're late,' he said. /"You're late," he said.*
They are also used in some kinds of writing:
– for quotations from a text, a famous speech etc.
– for some titles: *The Beatles' song 'Strawberry Fields Forever'*

Note that quotation marks:
– usually contain the words and the punctuation. (*'Her name's Tania.'*)
– are not used in reported speech
– can be single ('…') or double ("…") but the opening and closing mark must be the same.

Appendix 3
Spelling

Word endings

1 Plural nouns and present simple s
+ **-es** for words ending in -ch, -sh, -s, -ss, -x, -zz
→ wat**ches**, wa**shes**, bu**ses**, gla**sses**, bo**xes**, bu**zzes**

But note: potato → potat**oes**, tomato → tomat**oes**,
do → do**es**, go → go**es**

2 Consonant + -y
-y → -ies/-ier/-iest/-ily
sto**ry** → stor**ies**, f**ly** → fl**ies**, hap**py** → happ**ier**,
hea**vy** → heav**iest**, ang**ry** → angr**ily**

Note: **vowel** + -y: pl**ay** → pl**ays**/pl**ayed** (except l**ay** →
l**aid**, s**ay** → sa**id** and some adverbs: d**ay** → da**ily**)

3 One e before -ing
Remove e
lov**e** → lov**ing**, hop**e** → hop**ing** (but be → be**ing**;
double e: agre**e** → agr**ees**)

4 e before -ly
Keep e
polit**e** → polit**ely**
But note: tru**e** → tru**ly**; whol**e** → who**lly** and consonant
+ le: proba**ble** → proba**bly**; sensi**ble** → sensi**bly**

5 -c before -ed/-ing
-c → -ck
picni**c** → picni**cking**, pani**c** → pani**cked**

6 Nouns ending in -our
Remove u in adjective
hum**our** → hum**orous**

Doubling letters

1 Adjectives → adverbs
hopefu**l** → hopefu**lly**; carefu**l** → carefu**lly**

2 One-syllable words with one vowel + one consonant
sto**p** → sto**pping**/sto**pped**
ho**t** → ho**tter**/ho**ttest**

3 Two- or three-syllable words with the final syllable stressed
ad'**mit** → ad'mi**tted**; be'gin → be'gi**nning**

But note words with:
– two vowels + consonant (ch**eap** → che**ap**er,
  s**eem** → see**med**)
– two final consonants (sho**rt** → sho**rtest**; sta**rt** → sta**rted**)
– -y, -w, -x (st**ay** → st**aying**; ne**w** → ne**wer**; fa**x** → fa**xed**)
– two- or three- syllable words with the final syllable **not**
  stressed ('enter → 'enter**ing**, 'open → 'open**ed**)
(However, in British English, verbs with -l/-p **are** doubled:
'trave**l** → trave**lling**/trave**lled**, handica**p** → handica**pped**)

Some useful rules

1 i before e except after c (for long ee sounds)
bel**ie**ve, f**ie**ld, c**ei**ling
But note other sounds: for**ei**gn, l**ei**sure, th**ei**r, w**ei**gh

2 -ise (verb) /-ice (noun)
pract**ise** (verb) pract**ice** (noun)

Words often misspelt

accommodation, address, advisable, affect (verb)/effect
(noun), anxious, approximate
biscuit, building, burglar, business, busy
circle, comparison, confident
definitely, development, different, disappoint
embarrass, exhausted
familiar, frequent
guarantee, guilty
heard
immediate, individual, interest
library, lovable
medicine, misspell
necessary, noticeable
occasion, occupation
permanent, pleasant, possession, professional, pronunciation
receive/receipt, recommend, responsible
sandwiches, scissors, separate, similar
technical, through
until
valuable

Appendix 4
Linking expressions

Addition (= more information)

Linking parts of a sentence: *in addition to, as well as*
In addition to/As well as traditional academic subjects, students can study newer subjects like travel and tourism.

Linking ideas across sentences: *in addition, furthermore, other than that, apart from that, besides, moreover, what's more*
Students can study traditional academic subjects like science and languages. *In addition/Furthermore/Moreover/What's more*, they can study newer subjects like travel and tourism.
I work from 9.00 am to 5.00 pm. *Other than that/Apart from that*, I work Monday, Wednesday and Friday evenings.
I don't mind taking the dog for a walk. *Besides*, I need the exercise.

Note: we can also use *and* to join the sentences:
I don't mind taking the dog for a walk *and besides* I need the exercise.

Contrast

Linking parts of a sentence: *although, (even) though, while, whereas, in spite of, despite*
I went shopping, *although/(even) though* I didn't have much money.
She looks about forty, *while/whereas* her husband looks over sixty.
I went to work *despite/in spite of* feeling ill. (+ *-ing*)
                   my illness. (+ noun)
                   the fact that I was ill.
                   (+ the fact that)

Linking ideas across sentences: *however, nevertheless, even so, on the other hand*
I went shopping. *However*, I didn't have much money.
Everybody told us how dangerous the mountain was. *Nevertheless/Even so*, we decided to climb it.
(On the one hand) We would like to move to a new town. *On the other hand*, we realize that we would miss all our friends.

Note: we can also use *but* to join sentences beginning *nevertheless, even so, nevertheless, on the other hand* (but not *however*):
Everybody told us how dangerous the mountain was *but nevertheless/even so*, we decided to climb it.
(On the one hand) We would like to move to a new town *but on the other hand*, we realize that we would miss all our friends.

Reason and result

Linking parts of a sentence: *because, as, since, so, because of*
I went to bed *because/as/since* I was tired. (= reason)
Because/As/Since I was tired, I went to bed.
I was tired *so* I went to bed. (= result)
We stayed at home *because of* the weather. (= a noun is the reason)

Linking ideas across sentences: *therefore, consequently, this means/meant that, as a result, owing to*
I was tired. *Therefore* I went to bed. (= result)
We were running short of petrol. *This meant that* we had to find a garage. (= result)
William spent most of his money in the first week. *Consequently/As a result/Owing to* this, he couldn't afford to go out for the rest of his holiday. (= result)

Note: we can also use *and* to join the sentences:
I was tired *and therefore* I went to bed.

Purpose

Linking parts of a sentence: *(in order) to, so that*
I'm learning English *(in order) to* get a better job.
                   so that I can get a better job.

Note:
1 Punctuation:
  What's more, However, etc.
  I don't mind taking the dog for a walk. Besides, I need the exercise.
  I don't mind taking the dog for a walk and besides I need the exercise.
2 Position
  I went to bed because I was tired. ✓
  Because I was tired I went to bed. ✓
  I was tired so I went to bed. ✓
  ~~So I went to bed I was tired.~~ ✗
  I was tired. *Therefore, I went* to bed. ✓
  I was tired. *I therefore went* to bed. ✓
  William spent most of his money in the first week. *Consequently, he couldn't* afford to go out for the rest of his holiday. ✓
  William spent most of his money in the first week. *He consequently couldn't* afford to go out for the rest of his holiday. ✓
  William spent most of his money in the first week. ~~*He as a result couldn't*~~ afford to go out for the rest of his holiday. ✗

Audioscript

These recordings are mostly in standard British English accents. Where a speaker has a different accent, it is added in brackets.

Please note that the recording numbers below match the track numbers on the audio CD.

Unit2

🔘2 (Magda = German)

Magda   Hi! This is Magda. Do you remember me? I worked for you for two years when I first came to the UK from Germany. You probably remember that I left because I got a job as an administrator in a language school. I don't think I ever told you, but later I went on to do a full-time MBA specializing in Marketing at Liverpool University. Well, I'm phoning to give you the good news – I got my MBA – and I want to thank you and everybody at Kingsway Travel for being so nice and helpful. I couldn't have done the course without that experience. I don't know who is still there but could you give everyone who knew me my best wishes? Particularly Louise. I worked very closely with her. I really don't know what I'm going to do next. Have a holiday and think about it probably. Anyway, best wishes to everyone. And once again, thank you. Bye.

Unit3

🔘3 (Jessica = Australian; Karen = American)

Jessica   When are you off to Baja California, Karen?

Karen   I don't know yet. Probably in August, for three weeks. I'm still looking for another woman to share the driving.

Jessica   Are you going in that old camper van of yours?

Karen   Yes.

Jessica   Well, good luck to you! I hope it doesn't break down. What sort of person are you looking for?

Karen   Somebody about my age – in their mid-twenties. Somebody a bit like me.

Jessica   You mean someone always on the move doing things.

Karen   No, I'm not like that on vacation. I'm quite laid-back. I enjoy a bit of swimming or cycling but what I really like is lying around on the beach watching the sun set.

Jessica   So you want a travel companion with an easy-going approach to life. Someone to enjoy the sights with. Does she have to speak Spanish?

Karen   No, I speak pretty good Spanish. Don't forget, I used to live in Argentina.

Jessica   So where are you going to find this other person?

Karen   I don't know. I thought of either putting a small ad in this lifestyle magazine I buy or putting an ad on the noticeboard at the gym. What do you think?

Jessica   I'm not sure really …

Unit4

🔘4 (Speaker = German)

Speaker   Well, first you've got to say which country you want the money sent to. Well, that's the US but you'd better write the United States out in full. Don't forget to use capital letters and write each letter in one of those boxes. Then write Detroit because that's where David lives. OK, you've filled in the next bit, so let's go on to David's details. No, don't put a cross there, it's a tick. Oh, he's not a Doctor or Professor or anything, is he? If so, we'd have to write a different abbreviation here. Right, his last name is Eriksson – that's E-R-I-K-S-S-O-N – and I don't think he's got a middle name so just leave that blank. Right. Now, you're sending a thousand dollars, so write that out here in full – again in capitals – then write it in numbers here. OK. They'll need to check the other person's identity, so you need to think of a question they could ask him. What about your wife's name? It's Sonia, isn't it? So write the question and the answer here. Any message: what about something like: 'This is the money for the deposit.' We haven't room for any more – they only allow us ten words. Then, don't forget to sign and date it, starting off with the day.

Unit5

🔘5 (Melinda = Australian; Kaya = South African)

Melinda   How's your trip to Rio going?

Kaya   Oh, fantastic. What a city!

Melinda   Lucky you! I'd love to go.

Kaya   It must be one of the most beautiful cities in the world.

Melinda   I've seen pictures of it from Sugar Loaf Mountain.

Kaya   Yes, you get a wonderful 360-degree view from there. You see the city, the bay, the whole lot.

Melinda   I read somewhere that it's a natural harbour.

Kaya   Yes, and the mountains go right down to the sea and those amazing beaches at Copacabana and Ipanema. In fact our hotel's right on Ipanema Beach – right round the corner from lots of restaurants and all the main bus routes.

Melinda   It sounds ideal.

Kaya   It is. We've been to all the main tourist sights – and on public transport too. It's very good.

Melinda   Go on then. Tell me about the beaches, and make me really jealous.

Kaya   Ah! Now you're talking – gorgeous white sand. Today we saw volleyball and soccer courts set up all along the beach.

Melinda   No wonder they're such good footballers!

Kaya   People here play a game they call foot-volley. What athleticism and coordination! Amazing!

Melinda   What's Rio like as a city?

Kaya   In some ways it feels like lots of other big cities – packed streets, lots of shops, tiled pavements – clean. But here people spend a lot of time on the beach and at night you can dance to live samba music on the street!

Melinda   That sounds fun. Oh, lucky you! I do wish I was with you.

Kaya   But really it's the people I like most. This country has lots of different races and not one dominates, or so it seems. People are very warm – very genuine.

Unit7

6 (Customer Services Adviser = North American; Rhea = Indian)

Adviser   International Electronics. Good morning. How can I help you?

Rhea   Good morning.

Adviser   Hello.

Rhea   Yes, I bought a camera from you last month. I've just got my credit card bill and you've charged me 150 dollars – but when I bought it it was on special offer at 99 dollars.

Adviser   Ah, OK. How did you make the order? Was it on the web?

Rhea   Yes, it was.

Adviser   May I have your name?

Rhea   Yes, it's Rhea Gambhir.

Adviser   How do you spell your name?

Rhea   R-H-E-A G-A-M-B-H-I-R.

Adviser   Thanks. What day did you make the order?

Rhea   I'm not sure – about the 21st I think.

Adviser   What is the date on the credit card?

Rhea   The 23rd.

Adviser   Do you have an order number?

Rhea   No, I'm sorry, I don't.

Adviser   OK, well, I'll have to look into this and get back to you. I'll have a word with our order department. Could I have your phone number?

Rhea   Yes, I'm phoning from India and the number is 0091 22 2202 5516.

Adviser   Thanks, I'll get back to you later in the day.

Rhea   Thanks.

Unit8

7

Speaker   As we've got a new social activities organizer starting work on Monday, Head Office wants us to send an email telling him what's got to be done and when during the week. If you could make some notes on this timetable and then send him an email, I'd be very grateful.

OK, let's start with Monday. Well, that's when the new students arrive and we have our welcome in the morning before they go to classes. Obviously, we'll want him to be there and introduce himself – maybe indicate the kind of things that are on in the week, but that's not so important. The students will be too tired to take much information in. For the rest of the day, he'll need to get the reception ready for the evening – he'll have to pop out and get food and drink, things like that.

Tuesday is when the students are told about the week's activities, so that's when he goes round the classes and tells them what's on. As it's a fairly quiet day otherwise, he ought to spend the rest of the day planning the following week's activities. After classes, there's a guided walk around the city, showing them things like the post office, banks, etc. so I hope he knows where they are!

On Wednesday, there are always two things happening after school, either something in the school like a quiz, or a sports activity like tennis. He needs to find out which students want to do what, check that he's got staff available – maybe the teachers – and book things like tennis courts.

Thursday's barbecue day, which he'll need to plan carefully, and also the day when he needs to start thinking about the weekend excursion. He needs to put up a sheet so that students who want to go can sign up.

On Friday, he should take the sheets down and check the names and numbers of who wants to go, get deposits from the students and give the tour company a ring to tell them how many are coming. Oh, yes, he must check that there's a tour guide available – last summer I remember the students got there once and there was no tour guide. They said we hadn't booked one.

Then Saturday of course he will have to go with them to make sure that everything runs smoothly. It's very important that he meets up with the tour guide and introduces the students.

Well, that's all I can think of. I'll let you know if there's anything else.

Unit9

8 (Lin Ting = Chinese; Ilya = Russian; Roberto = Spanish)

Tom   I think it should be quite a big event really. Both of them have been on the staff a very long time and gave a lot to the company. Without them the company would be quite different.

Judy   I don't know. We've had other members of staff leave recently – and some of those were with us a long time – and we didn't have a big leaving party for them.

Tom   That's true, but a lot of people commented afterwards that they thought we should have done a lot more for them. It looked a bit mean.

Lin Ting   OK, when shall we have it?

Ilya   Not on the last Friday of the month – too many people will be away.

Tom   What about the Wednesday? Roberto?

Roberto   Yes, that's OK. I was thinking of lunch time.

Lin Ting   Do you think that's a good idea? It'd be much more relaxed in the evening, and people could stay as long as they want.

Roberto   OK.

Judy   And let's lay on a good buffet with drinks. Will you make a speech, Roberto?

Roberto   If I have to.

Lin Ting   Who shall we invite? Ex-members of staff as well as present staff?

Judy   I'm not sure that's a good idea. There are quite a few people who were made redundant last year and they're still very upset.

Roberto   True. OK, present members of staff only.

Ilya   And their partners …

Roberto   And their partners as it's in the evening.

Lin Ting   Where shall we hold it?

Judy   In the main reception area would be best. And let's use outside caterers for the food – it would save a lot of mess and washing up.

Roberto   I agree …

Judy   Now one of us ought to be responsible for organizing all this. What about you, Tom?

Tom   Me? I'm far too busy …

Judy   Ilya?
Ilya   I don't mind, as long as everyone else gives me a hand.
Everyone   Of course … Of course …

🔵 **9** (Beatriz = Brazilian; Gary = Canadian; Riko = Japanese; Yusuf = Egyptian)
Beatriz   Cheap air travel is great for our generation. It means we get to see much more of the world than my parents' generation.
Gary   Yeah, but there is a big downside. Some places get so swamped with the tourists that they destroy the very places they've come to see. They trample over the environment, put up huge hotels and destroy the culture of the place.
Riko   Oh, I don't think so. Tourists bring in a lot of money and there are a lot of roads and other facilities that wouldn't get built otherwise.
Gary   Who wants the natural world covered with tarmac and great big international hotels!
Beatriz   A lot of the locals, actually. It means that they have jobs and an income they otherwise wouldn't have.
Gary   Oh, yes, all very low incomes, very seasonal, without job security – and most of the real money goes outside to the big international chains, the hotel groups, the airlines, the international developers, the travel agents … Most of the bosses are foreign.
Yusuf   Why is it then that some countries depend on tourism as their main source of income?
Beatriz   Some countries organize themselves better than others and these days there's a lot more awareness of the need for more environmentally friendly tourism – eco-tourism …
Gary   That's all very idealistic! Most tourists don't care about that. They don't really respect local customs or learn the language – they just want a nice holiday in the sun …
Yusuf   What's wrong with that? …
Gary   Take pictures or have a holiday villa built.
Yusuf   Well, that helps the local economy.
Gary   Does it?
Yusuf   I think you are being too negative. A lot of young people nowadays try and integrate much more than their parents, use local shops and traders, local accommodation, and are interested in preserving local customs …
Gary   Maybe … I think there needs to be much greater legal protection to try and preserve the environment and wildlife, as well as the rights of local workers, and to make sure not all the money disappears out of the country.
Riko   I think the best way is not legal protection but through education to make people much more aware of different cultures and customs …
Gary   I agree with that.

Unit 10

🔵 **10** (Passenger 1 = Irish; Passenger 2 = Australian; Customer 1 = Indian; Customer 2 = Irish)
Situation A
Announcer   Flight AA7676 to Dubai is ready for boarding from Gate Number 3.
Attendant   Did you pack your bags yourself or did somebody pack them for you?
Passenger 1   No, I packed them myself.
Passenger 2   There's our bag. Quick. Go and get it.
Passenger 3   I'm sorry, but can I have a word with you?

Situation B
Customer 1   Two nights. No smoking, please.
Customer 2   Excuse me, I'd like to see the manager.

🔵 **11** (Rick = Australian)
Rick   I'm sorry to trouble you but I thought I'd better give you a ring. I don't know if you heard but on Monday we tried to book two of our team onto the Human Resources workshop you ran yesterday. I know we left it a bit late but the person we spoke to said it shouldn't be a problem and took their names. We assumed everything was OK, so the guys turned up only to be told that they weren't on the list and there weren't any places left. Well, you can imagine they weren't very pleased – and to be honest neither was I. I gather there was a bit of an argument at the door. I can't remember who it was I spoke to in the first place and I suppose I should have been a bit worried that we had no email confirmation and no one asked us to pay a deposit, but I never thought this would happen. Anyway I thought I'd better tell you. Up to now we've always been very happy with your courses and there have never been any problems. I'm sure it was just a one-off. All the same it was a bit annoying.

Unit 11

🔵 **12** (Mr Zhirkov = Russian)
Mr Zhirkov   I tried to phone you at your office today but you were out. They gave me your phone number at home. I hope you don't mind. Just to say I'm very pleased that you will be coming to Moscow. You will be able to look round the company and we will be able to talk about some of the details of our business deal. In your email you said your plane arrives in the afternoon of Monday 4th of August at 4.30. Why don't I come and meet you at the airport? We could discuss your programme in the car and I'll take you to the company. I don't know if you're planning a meeting with one of your banks while you're here. But never mind. Perhaps you could email me and tell me what you want me to do.

13 (Laurent = French; Mitsuko = Japanese)

Mitsuko Good morning. Travel Europa.

Laurent Hello, can I speak to Mitsuko, please?

Mitsuko Speaking.

Laurent Hello, Mitsuko. It's Laurent.

Mitsuko Oh, yes, good morning.

Laurent I have been planning your trip to France and I have a possible itinerary for you. I haven't arranged everything yet because I want to see what you think.

Mitsuko Thank you. I'll just get a piece of paper. … Very good. I'm ready.

Laurent All right. On March the first you get the Eurostar – the train from the UK to France – from London at 7.09 in the morning. I'm sorry, it's a little early but …

Mitsuko No, no.

Laurent OK, so you get to Paris at 10.59 local time, and we will organize a coach to take the students to their hostel. It's called the Boissière.

Mitsuko Sorry?

Laurent Boissière. That's spelt B-O-I-S-S-I-E-R-E (you, you can find it on the Internet if you are interested). I don't know if you want to stay there as well or do you want a better hotel? It will be more expensive, of course.

Mitsuko No, no. I want to be with the students.

Laurent OK. In the afternoon there will be a coach tour around Paris to look at the famous sights.

Mitsuko Eiffel Tower, Notre Dame …

Laurent Yes, yes, of course. And there will be a guide.

Mitsuko Very good.

Laurent OK. Now you said you wanted me to organize some classes in French history and culture. Well, I have spoken to some schools and there will be no problem but I haven't decided where yet. 'TBA' as we say – to be arranged.

Mitsuko Excellent.

Laurent So that's four days, from the second to the fifth. The classes will be in the morning, and in the afternoon you will visit art galleries, places of historical interest …

Mitsuko The Louvre, Versailles …

Laurent Yes, of course. On the morning of the sixth you will take the fast train – the TGV – from Paris to Avignon. Of course, we will have a coach to meet you at the station and take you to a nice little hotel near the centre. I haven't booked anything yet but there, er, won't be a problem. TBA …

Mitsuko TBA …

Laurent Well. In the afternoon you will visit the wonderful palace in Avignon and see the famous bridge … OK, the next two days …

Mitsuko The seventh and eighth?

Laurent Yes. You will have a coach tour of the South of France. I haven't arranged it yet but you will see the beautiful countryside, the coast, historical sites, museums, art galleries, gardens … Everything!

Mitsuko Wonderful. TBA …

Laurent Exactly. And, the next day, nearly your last, I thought it would be nice to have a trip to Monaco.

Mitsuko Monaco!

Laurent Yes, it's very beautiful and we can arrange for your students to attend one or two lectures at the International University there. I'm sure they will find it very interesting.

Mitsuko That sounds good.

Laurent OK, the last day, we take you back by coach to Nice and you fly back to the UK from there. OK?

Mitsuko OK. Yes, everything sounds just fine …

Unit 12

14 (Student A = Chinese; Student B = Indian; Student C = Italian; Student D = New Zealander; Student E = Brazilian)

Student A Yes, I use the swimming pool but it's only 15 metres long, far too small. It gets very crowded and when it's busy you can't really swim. One college I've been to has an Olympic-size pool which is 50 metres long!

Student B The sports hall? It's a joke! What can you do there? Only netball and volleyball. I'm in the badminton club and we have to use the courts in town. And it's far too small for things like five-a-side football. The university needs to spend some serious money – we need a real sports hall desperately.

Student C The gym? Great!

Staff Member A Yes, I like the gym. It's got about 100 fitness stations I think, so it's big enough.

Student D Yes, I like the gym too.

Staff Member B Tennis? No, I never use the courts. Every time I try they're booked solid. There are only three. And the students who use them complain – they say they're in a bad way. They need repairing. I don't know what they mean by that – you'd have to ask them.

Student E The tennis courts? Oh, no. They're in a terrible state. The university needs to spend a lot of money on them – and we need more.

Unit 13

15

Presenter Two films which best illustrate the horror genre of more recent years are *Psycho*, made in 1960, and *The Blair Witch Project*, made in 1999.

Psycho has been described as the 'mother of all modern horror suspense films', although that title might not be quite accurate since most critics see it as more of a psychological thriller than the kind of bloody horror film that came later. The film is about an office worker, Marion Crane, who steals $40,000 from her boss's client and drives all day to escape. As night falls in the pouring rain, she turns off the motorway and decides to spend the night at the isolated Bates Motel, run by a strange young man, Norman Bates, who seems to be obsessed by his mother. I won't give away the whole plot but then Norman serves Marion dinner and she goes back to her room for a shower. From that point on the fear and suspense increase and there is a horrific murder.

In one way, *The Blair Witch Project* is quite different in that it pretends to be an amateur movie. It is about three film students who travel to Maryland to make a student film about a local legend, the Blair Witch. The three go into the woods on a two-day trek to find the Blair Witch, and never come back. One year later, the students' video is found in the woods. Often there is a blank screen and all we hear is their scared cries and unexplained noises.

🔊 **16** (Presenter = American)

Presenter More than 150,000 people followed the body of Dr Martin Luther King, Jr to burial in Atlanta. Among the mourners were the President's wife, Jacqueline Kennedy, and the Vice President, Hubert Humphrey.
Anticipating his own death, in his last sermon Dr King had asked that he be remembered because he 'gave his life for love'.
Dr King was shot dead by the white assassin, James Earl Ray, while standing on a hotel balcony. Within hours of his death, there were riots in dozens of towns throughout the US.

News announcer Today, the 11th of February, is a historic day in the history of South Africa. It is the day on which the great anti-apartheid leader, Nelson Mandela, has been freed from prison after 27 years. Dressed in a light brown suit and tie, he appeared holding the hand of his wife Winnie, smiled at the ecstatic crowds and punched the air in a victory salute. Across the country people have been dancing in the streets. In his speech to the nation at a rally in Cape Town, he has declared his commitment to peace and reconciliation with the country's white minority, but made it clear that the ANC's armed struggle is not yet over. His main aim is to bring peace to the black majority and give them the right to vote in both national and local elections.

Unit 14

🔊 **17** (Samir = Indian)

Ben What's it like working on your own?

Samir Not so bad now, but I found it quite difficult at first.

Ben Why? What was the problem?

Samir Well, you quickly realize that everything is down to you. If you don't work, you don't get paid.

Ben But that's true about working for somebody else, isn't it?

Samir Not really. At the office I used to work at, I had good days and bad days. On the bad days I still got paid. Also, when I was sick, I got sick pay, which you don't get when you're working on your own. When you work on your own you miss the regular payments going into your bank. You have to be responsible for yourself. Nobody's going to look after you and you've got very few legal rights.

Ben So why did you do it then?

Samir Well, there are lots of advantages. For a start, your time's your own, you can make your own choices and you've got a lot of freedom. If you feel like taking a day off or going to the gym in the middle of the day, you can. Also, as I'm working from home, I get to see the family.

Ben Is that always a good thing?

Samir Not always, to be honest. Sometimes it's difficult to break from work to be with the family, and sometimes the kids get in the way when you're trying to work. The most important thing is you have to be disciplined. You have to be able to organize yourself and your time and have a routine, and your family have to respect that or it doesn't work.

Ben Yes, I can see that. But just think, you don't have to commute hours to work like I do.

Samir That's true. I don't miss that! And really, when working on your own goes well, it's really satisfying. But be warned – you often have to work a lot harder!

Unit 15

🔊 **18** (Jo = Australian)

Jo Sorry, Sophie. I was stuck in the corner and couldn't see the screen very well. And there was a very tall student in front of me too. Did you manage to get down all the figures? I could ask the lecturer for a printout but I've only got one or two numbers missing.

Sophie Sure. No problem. What are you missing?

Jo OK. First, the number of hours a week that the over-60s watch TV.

Sophie Mmm, yes, this is a surprise when you compare it with the other age groups. It's 30 hours.

Jo Really? That's interesting. Um, what about the time spent playing on computers for the 22- to 39-year-olds?

Sophie Oh, that's not a surprise. It's up like the others. 6.25 – six and a quarter hours.

Jo Yeah, I suppose we're all computer-mad these days. What about the cinema habits of the 13- to 21-year-olds?

Sophie Oh that's down to 0.75 per week. Only three-quarters of an hour on average.

Jo That's sad. What about sport for the 40- to 60-year-olds?

Sophie 2.5 – two and a half hours – which makes the over-60s the exception to the rule!

Jo That's true. And are they the exception to the rule in socializing?

Sophie Yes, they are really, because there's been no change in their habits. Two and a half hours again!

Jo So that's still the same …

Sophie Do you need anything else?

Jo No, I think that's everything, thanks. Thanks a lot, Sophie. I think I'll sit with you next time!

Unit 16

🔊 **19** (Presenter = Irish)

Presenter Japan receives business travellers from around the world and the wise visitor will learn some local etiquette before setting off. Japanese culture is quite different to that of many countries and foreign visitors to Japan sometimes worry that, in their ignorance of the country's social etiquette, they may appear rude or cause offence during their stay. However, with a few useful tips, you can easily avoid giving offence.
The first thing to consider is appearance. What should you wear? In most situations, the Japanese dress according to their status or position and casual dress is therefore not appropriate for business travellers. Men should wear dark business suits while women should wear conservative dress and try and avoid too many accessories. Also, remember the Japanese don't wear outside shoes inside the house or in many restaurants, so it's a good idea to have footwear that's easy to remove.
Let's now look at business entertaining. Your hosts may bring up the idea of getting together socially after your formal meetings. This may be a sincere invitation to dinner, but it might just be polite talk and you shouldn't be offended if the dinner is never mentioned again. Japanese business people rarely entertain at home and normally any entertaining takes place in restaurants or bars after business hours.
In Japan, gifts are always appreciated, particularly at the end of a visit. Before you leave your home country, consider bringing a

small souvenir that represents the place where you live and give it to your host. Make sure that your gift is stylishly wrapped in tasteful colours, not white, which symbolizes death, or bright colours. When you give and accept the gift, use both hands.

When you're in a business meeting, remember the Japanese do not 'talk' with their hands so avoid using large hand gestures, unusual facial expressions and any dramatic movements which could draw attention to yourself. Another sign of respect is to take notes at a meeting. This will show that you are interested and will be appreciated by your hosts. Like gifts, the Japanese give and receive business cards with both hands and you should take special care in handling them. Examine any business card you receive carefully and don't write on it, as this will be seen as a sign of disrespect.

If all this sounds a little daunting, don't worry. Japanese people are aware that their ways are unfamiliar to foreigners and most will happily overlook any unintended social mistakes or, or politely point them out. Above all, the most important thing to remember is that part of the attraction of visiting Japan is experiencing its unique and fascinating culture.

Review 2

20 (Chef = Italian)

Chef OK, I'll tell you how to cook the kind of rice and bean soup they serve in Venice.

The first thing to remember is that you need to wash the dried beans and leave them to soak about 12 hours beforehand because they're not washed before they're stored. Use cold tap water, leave to soak as I said, and then drain them. Let's make the recipe for about 200 grams of beans, OK? Right, we're ready to start cooking. Get hold of a saucepan and heat 3 tablespoons of olive oil and a knob of butter (about 50 grams). While you're doing that, chop half an onion and then sauté it in the oil and butter with a piece of smoked bacon, chopped into small bits – about 50 grams' worth. Do that for a few minutes, then put in the beans and cover them with plenty of water. Bring it to the boil, then put the lid on and cook it on a moderate heat for … mmm … about two hours.

Just before the two hours are up, get 300 grams of long-grain rice ready and half a litre of hot beef stock. Pour the whole lot into the mix and leave it on the heat until the rice is cooked. The soup should be quite liquid. Finally, season it with salt and pepper according to how you like it.

21 (Travel agent = South African)

Travel agent Hi, just to let you know I've started to get together an itinerary for your holiday in South Africa. This is very much a first draft and I've only looked at the first few days so far, but I thought I'd give you a ring just to get your reaction.

You'll arrive on the Monday at Port Elizabeth Airport, which is known locally as the 'ten-minute' airport because it's no more than ten minutes to the most important places and in fact only five minutes to the beach. There you'll collect your hire car and drive to the Park Inn Hotel. I'll let you have details later.

Then on Tuesday you drive the 100 kilometres to St Francis Bay. You'll check in to your hotel, which is the Oasis Lodge Hotel – Oasis, that's O-A-S-I-S – and relax, look around, whatever you like.

Wednesday is the activity day. There are lots to choose from. You can go walking, play golf, go fishing, do water sports. It's up to you. I'll give you some options.

On Thursday, what I'm thinking is that I'll organize a day tour of a lion park and an elephant park. The elephant park is incredible – it's only about, er, 90 minutes away from St Francis Bay but there are more elephants there per square kilometre than anywhere else in the world. In the evening we'll take you back to the hotel for dinner.

Then on Friday there'll be a day visit to a game farm, which has rhinos, giraffes and buffalo. You'll be able to go round by jeep, on horseback or mountain bike, as you wish.

Anyway, that's all so far. Let me know what you think. If there's anything you want me to add in, just let me know …

Answer key

Unit 1

Get ready to write
- *Your own answer.*
- *Your own answer.*
- *Your own answers. Possible answers:*
  - a   it's cheaper
  - b   the programme is inflexible
  - c   finding enough rooms for everyone / trying to find something to suit everyone

A

1   c

2   b T   c T   d T   e F (the email has some more formal language)

3   b   reasonably priced   c   require   d   offer us a special rate   e   inform me

4   a   No   b   To get information   c   Neutral

5   Paragraph 1 – saying why you're writing
Paragraph 2 – asking about facilities
Paragraph 3 – saying how long you want to stay; asking about price (it is often better to ask other questions before asking about the price);
Paragraph 4 – final comment
Paragraph 5 – closing the email

Focus on functional and fixed expressions

Your own answers. Possible answers:

1   2 g   3 b   4 e   5 f   6 a   7 c

2   (I saw your advertisement) in the newspaper.
(I look forward to receiving) this information as soon as possible.

3   Best wishes. ('Yours faithfully' is more commonly used in very formal letters; 'Cheers' is too informal; 'Goodbye' is not a closing salutation in writing.)

6   *Your own answer. Possible answer:*

I recently saw your advertisement in *The Herald* offering an apartment for rent in Venice. I am very interested in coming next July with my partner but before I make a booking I have a number of questions I would like to ask.

You say the apartment is beautifully designed but I need to know a bit about the facilities. For example, is there air-conditioning, which will be very important in July? Also, I need an internet connection because I have to check my emails while I'm away.

I notice that it is possible to make a booking for less than a week. We are planning to stay for four nights in early July. I assume that would be acceptable. Could you give me some idea of the price for this length of stay at that time of the year?

I look forward to receiving this information as soon as possible so that I can make an early booking.

Best wishes

Extra practice

2   *Your own answer. Possible answer:*

I have seen your advertisement offering b&b accommodation and am very interested.

This December I'm planning to be in the San Francisco Bay area on a walking holiday and I am looking for suitable places to stay on my route.

You don't say exactly where you are located. Could you give me precise details and also tell me the minimum number of nights I can stay. Is it possible to stay for just one night?

I'm delighted to see that your bedrooms have a fireplace. You also say that most rooms have a Jacuzzi. It would be wonderful if I could have a room with one.

Also, I will be travelling with a friend and we would want to share a room. Do all your rooms accommodate two people and is the price per person or for the room? Is there an extra charge for breakfast if there are two people?

My final question is when do I have to book? My plans are not yet certain and I might not know until about a month before I arrive. Would you still have rooms free then?

I look forward to hearing from you as soon as possible.

Unit 2

Get ready to write
- *Your own answers. Possible answers:*
  - a   email (because phoning might be too familiar and a letter too formal/impractical)
  - b   phone (or possibly email)
  - c   letter because it manages to keep a distance and you don't have to show your disappointment!
- a   ✓✓ (polite)
  - b   ✓ (as it's a friend it's not necessary to be polite but it's important to be friendly, enthusiastic and grateful)
  - c   ✓✓✓ (very polite because you don't want to offend your relative)

A

1   2 G   3 F   4 C   5 B   6 H   7 A   8 E

2   You write your home address in the top right-hand corner. In business letters you may write the address of the person you are writing to on the left starting below your address. The date is usually beneath the lower address.

3   give formal thanks to the staff of a company.

4   The style is polite and formal because Mr Korsimbi is a very important person and not a close friend of Tom's.

5   a   Section C   b   Section F   c   Section B

6   a

7 *Your own answers. Possible answers*:

 b   As a result of your kindness and generosity…

 c   Their hospitality and general support were a great comfort to us…

 d   … please give our appreciation and thanks to all concerned.

9 a   The letter will be quite polite and friendly.

 b   *Your own answers*.

10 *Your own answers.*

Focus on polite phrases

1 b   I know how much you … *loved working there.*

 c   I hope this doesn't mean that … *you'll be without work for too long.*

 d   On a positive note … *it means you'll be able to spend more time with your family.*

 e   Please let me know if … *you'd like me to look after the children.*

2 *Take care of yourself* is the most respectful. It shows sympathy and support. However, *I wish you the very best* would also be acceptable. *Yours sincerely* and *Yours faithfully* are too formal, and *Yours faithfully* is normally only used when we do not know the name of the person we're writing to.

---

11 *Your own answer. Possible answer*:

Dear Dave

I'm really sorry to hear that you are losing your job along with all the other workers at Sweetline. I know how much you loved working there and you must feel very bitter that they are closing the factory down, having promised only last month that the factory had a bright future.

I hope this doesn't mean that you will be without work for too long. I read in the paper that the company is helping workers find alternative employment. I know it will be difficult in the short term because of your children but presumably the government will give you some support while you are looking for another job. On a positive note, it means that for a period at least you will be able to spend a bit more time with them at home.

Remember that you and I have known each other for a long time and I will do anything I can to help you. Please let me know if you'd like me to look after the children at any time or if there is any support I can give.

Take care of yourself
Debbie

13 b   (G) last month   c   (V) job   d   (P) you'd

 e   (WO) look after the children   f   (VF) doesn't

B

2 *Your own answer. Possible answer*:

On behalf of everyone here at Kingsway Travel Agency, I would like to congratulate you on your MBA.

I must say I was not surprised you have done so well. During your first year as an employee with us I noted how bright you are and how you have a very quick mind for business. If you put those qualities together with your strong work ethic, your commitment to quality customer service, and your ability to work with and inspire others, it is obvious that you have a great future ahead of you. I am glad that you feel that your experience working with us contributed in some small way to your success.

I have passed on your best wishes to the staff, in particular Louise, who is still with us. They all say they miss you and hope you will call in to see them sometime. Once again, congratulations on your success, and I wish you all the best in your future career whatever it may be.

Wishing you all the best

Focus on word choice

 b   very bright: *very intelligent*

 c   ability to work with and inspire others: *a good team-player and shows some leadership qualities*

 d   strong work ethic: *works extremely hard*

 e   quality customer service: *a first-class service to the customer*

Unit3

Get ready to write

○ *Your own answers. Possible answers*:

 a   To sell small domestic items or to find/offer local accommodation.

 b   For similar purposes but to a wider audience.

○ *Your own answers.*

○ *Your own answer. Possible answer*:

It should give the necessary information in few words.

A

1 b   1   c   3   d   2

2 b   very good condition   c   minutes   d   per week

 e   including   f   number

3 b   4   c   1   d   3

4 3 is longer with no words left out or abbreviations.

 Advantages: it is clear and contains a lot of information.

 Disadvantages: some readers wouldn't have the patience to read it.

5 supporting information 2; contact details 3

6 A   a flat   B   his/her English   C   a family cat

7 All these except *add in extra information* (there is enough there already) and *make the sentences longer* (they need to be made shorter and easy to read).

8 *Your own answers. Possible answers*:

 a   ~~I am a~~ former lecturer from ~~the~~ University of Sydney ~~and for the four weeks of~~ July ~~I am~~ returning to Sydney with ~~my new~~ wife. ~~I want to~~ rent a flat, preferably in or near Darlington. ~~I'd be really pleased if you were able to~~ email me with offers at hhiggins@div.cam.edu.

 b   Uni, pref, nr

9 second: what is being offered.

 third: contact details.

10 By highlighting key information and leaving out words where possible. At present the advertisement is too wordy and chatty. Examples: Ginger long-haired male. V. timid. BIG REWARD!!!

11 *Your own answers. Possible answers*:

 A   FLAT RENTAL WANTED 4 WKS JULY Pref. in/nr Darlington. Former Sydney Uni lecturer hoping return for visit with wife hhiggins@div.cam.edu

 B   Postgrad. student from Beijing wants to improve English speaking. Offers English–Chinese language exchange. 06784-63109

 C   LOST!!! Family cat. Ginger long-haired male. V. timid. Disappeared 7/4. Greatly missed. Reward $50. Mobile: 0478-666-111

Answer key

Extra practice 1

1 a her, mid-twenties b relaxed and easy-going
   c doesn't have to d should e should
2 swimming, cycling, lying around on the beach, looking at local sights
3 *Your own answers.*
5 *Your own answer. Possible answer*:
   TRAVEL COMPANION WANTED FOR 3-WEEK VACATION IN BAJA CALIFORNIA IN AUGUST. Woman in mid-twenties (likes swimming, cycling, lying around on the beach - speaks Spanish) seeks easy-going female companion to share driving in old camper van and enjoy the sights with. Contact Karen on (619) 299-7683.

Extra practice 2

Your own answer. Possible answer:
(FOUND) – Car keys for luxury car in the Castle Hill area. Keys have metal badge with a logo. Identify them and we will return them. Please come to Reception at Shelley's Bookshop.

Unit 4

Get ready to write

○ *Your own answers.*
○ *Your own answers.*
○ *Your own answers.*

A

1 b 4 c 1 d 2
2 Form 1 was completed online.
3 a No, she is single.
   b She wants a single account.
4 a She comes from Japan.
   b She wants executive accommodation.
   c She will pay her fees by credit card.
5 a 102,110 miles.
   b It will start from May.
6 a They are 24 and 23 years old.
   b He follows a *halal* diet.
7 a after *First name* and *Surname* in form 4
   b after *Make and model* in form 3

Focus on writing numbers in words

a 13th *thirteenth*   13 *thirteen*
b 30th *thirtieth*   31st *thirty-first*
c 4th *fourth*   14th *fourteenth*
d 1st *first*   12th *twelfth*
e 9th *ninth*   99 *ninety-nine*
f 25 *twenty-five*   25th *twenty-fifth*
g 8th *eighth*   88 *eighty-eight*
h 2nd *second*   22nd *twenty-second*
i Four hundred and fifty dollars
j One thousand, one hundred and fifteen pounds and thirteen pence
k two hundred and seventy-five euros

8 b 5 c 1 d 2 e 4
9 a Individually b Yes
11

Send Form — *PLEASE COMPLETE IN BLOCK CAPITALS*

DESTINATION
Country UNITED STATES
City DETROIT
Is there a suitable receive agent at the above destination? If not please ask staff to confirm

RECEIVER
Title (please tick) Mr. ✓ Mrs. Ms. Miss. Other (please state)
First Name DAVID
Middle Name
Surname ERIKSSON

TRANSACTION
Amount to be sent (In words and figures) ONE THOUSAND DOLLARS
In figures $1000
Test Question WHAT IS MY WIFE'S NAME?
Answer SONIA
Message (Max 10 words) THIS IS THE MONEY FOR THE DEPOSIT.

Unit 5

Get ready to write

○ *Your own answers.*
○ *Your own answers.*

A

1 friends B   grandparents A
2 a less b more c less
3 'very cool place' ; 'you guys'
4 give the context by saying where you are
5 a *Hi all* b *Hello Grandma and Grandpa*
6 talks about where the person is going next – 4
   gives general impressions – 2
   talks about disadvantages – 3
7 a really, really tiny b we do get a lot of (instead of we get …)
   c so peaceful; so relaxed d amazingly beautiful
8 *Your own answers. Possible answers*:
   a I am writing to a friend.
   b several adjectives to describe a few specific details.
   c the general context (where I am and what I'm doing).
   d the key features of the place(s).
   e where I am going next.

1   How are you? After I left you in Cape Town, I decided to get a cheap flight to New Zealand because I wanted to walk along the Milford Track. Have you heard about it?

2   Luckily, we were blessed with sunny weather, which is amazing since Mackinnon Pass is one of the wettest places on Earth. Unfortunately, on the last day the weather broke and it poured down and was quite cold.

9   *Your own answer. Possible answer*:

Although I took lots of pictures I know that none of the pictures will do the place justice. I'll just have to keep everything in my memory. My regret was that you weren't there with me. You would have loved the whole trek. Anyway, from here I'm planning to travel a bit more around South Island.

10   *Your own answer. Possible answer*:

How are you, Areefa? After I left you in Cape Town, I decided to get a cheap flight to New Zealand because I wanted to do the Milford Track. Have you heard about it? It's a four-day, 53.5km walk in some of the most spectacular areas of natural beauty in the world and you stay in huts along the way.

Luckily, the first day was an easy walk, mainly along the flat and the weather was very calm. On the second day we walked 16km, which was quite exhausting, but we got incredible views of the valley and the beautiful turquoise-colour river which runs through it. The next day we walked to the top of Mackinnon Pass, and the views from the top were simply stunning. Fortunately, we were blessed with sunny weather, which is amazing since this is one of the wettest places on Earth! Unfortunately, on the last day the weather broke and it poured down and was quite cold. It was great to see the valley though, as all the waterfalls suddenly appeared. The whole area was covered by mist and cloud and was very mysterious and still.

Although I took lots of pictures I know that none of the pictures will do the place justice. I'll just have to keep everything in my memory. My regret was that you weren't there with me. You would have loved the whole trek. Anyway, from here I'm planning to travel a bit more around South Island.

B

1   *Your own answers.*

2   *Your own answers.*

3   *Your own answer. Possible answer*:

Rio is one of the most beautiful cities in the world. To really appreciate the setting you should go up Sugar Loaf Mountain, where you'll get a 360-degree view of Rio and Guanabara Bay. You'll see how the natural harbour is surrounded by high mountains that meet the sea in the world-famous beaches of Copacabana and Ipanema.

Our hotel in Rio is right on Ipanema Beach and couldn't be better placed. It is just round the corner from restaurants and major bus routes. Of course we do the obvious sights, mostly by public transport.

The beaches are wonderful. Just today we went down to the gorgeous white sand to find volleyball and soccer courts set up all along the beach. People here play a game they call foot-volley. It's the most amazing display of athleticism and coordination I've ever seen.

For me, Rio is much the same as many big cities in Spain. The streets are packed with people and shops, the pavements are clean and tiled. The only difference is that here you spend a lot of time on the beach or dance to live samba on the street at night! One of the things I like most is the people. Brazil is a country with lots of different races and no one race dominates. People really are genuinely warm.

Unit 6

Get ready to write

○   a   2 ('sandwiches are outstanding' 'open all night' 'great BBQ')
     b   1 ('played over 80 hours' 'fun it provides')

○   *Your own answer.*

A

1   a   On a DVD seller's website.
        b   No – it's probably a customer's review.

2   a   catches the reader's attention
        b   makes it clear what the film is about
        c   gives the main reasons for enjoying the film
        d   expresses some reservations about the film
        e   gives a personal recommendation

3   b   utterly   c   fairly   d   completely   e   practically

4   b   though (*though* means the same as *although* but is informal; it can also be used at the end of a sentence, unlike *although*. *Even so* means 'despite what has just been said' and usually begins a sentence)

        c   Even more (*even more* is an expression used to emphasize a comparison – *even more disappointing than the film ending in 1968. Moreover* is a formal word used to add information, meaning 'also and more importantly'); All the same; *All the same* is an informal expression meaning 'despite what has just been said'; *What's more* is an informal expression for *In addition*)

5   a   To recommend the book   b   fairly informal

6   *Your own answers.*

Focus on linking expressions

b   However, such as   c   Besides   d   In addition
e   Nevertheless   f   In fact

7   *Your own answer. Possible answer*:

I read this book without stopping and found it deeply inspiring and thought-provoking. I will remember forever Osmond's suggestion that we should stop looking for happiness and realize that we can't have happiness in life without unhappiness.

In the book, the author argues very strongly that happiness is not the same as pleasure and that the experience of happiness is different for each and every one of us. To support his argument he looks back through history and at the major religions of the world. There are useful links to interesting websites for anyone wanting to find out more.

My only complaint about the book is that it's a bit vague in places and doesn't give us a clear path to happiness as it suggests in the title. Also it's too short, given the importance of the subject.

But, all in all, if happiness is something that worries you, then this book is for you – you won't regret it!

Answer key

Extra practice

5 *Your own answer. Possible answer*:
Deal or No Deal ****

Deal or No Deal might be the silliest game show ever or the most brilliant in its simplicity. But it's certainly not a quiz show. It requires no knowledge of any subject; it's a game of pure chance, in which one player has to gamble with prize money. Here's how it works: a contestant must pick one numbered box from 26, not knowing how much is in it. Each case has a different amount of money, from $1 (Hong Kong) to $3 million (Hong Kong). The contestant calls out the numbers of the other cases and, one by one, they are opened and their amounts revealed. From time to time, a 'banker' makes an offer on the case originally chosen.

It is a simple idea and that is what makes the programme such compulsive viewing. To add to the attraction, the host makes us care about the contestants and whether they win or lose. The interaction between them can be hilarious, moving and frustrating in equal measures.

Some people find the show incredibly boring. Others hate it, saying that it is television at its worst. At least in quiz shows there's always something you can learn from the questions, but there aren't even any questions here.

However, this show is already a big hit in over 40 countries around the world. Can so many people be wrong?

Review 1

A

1 b (e.g. I am particularly interested in the one …)
2 a (e.g. First, let me say that …)
3–5 I have seen on your website that you have villas to rent in the south of Portugal. (1) I am particularly interested in the one with the Reference No. P2710 and would like some more details. (2)

First, let me say that we are coming with another family and we're looking for a place which will sleep 10 people. (3) However, the villa we're interested in only has four bedrooms. (4) Could you tell me how many beds there are in each? (5)

My next point is that we are planning to come in July, which is probably your busiest period. (6) At this stage we don't know the exact dates, but I should know shortly. (7) In the meantime, could you tell me what availability you have? (8)

Lastly, I'd like to know something about the location. (9) One of the things that attracts me to the villa is that it is close to the beach and has spectacular views. (10) However, the one thing that worries me is that it might be a bit noisy at night if there are nightclubs nearby. (11) Are there any that I need to be worried about? (12)

Thank you in advance. (13) I look forward to hearing from you. (14)

B

Your own answer. Possible answer:
FOR SALE PENTIUM 3 LAPTOP 20 Gig. HD vgc. with free laptop bag. Only £600!!! 07645-732651

C

VISA DEPARTMENT

Please complete the application form in CAPITAL LETTERS and BLACK INK.

Title: Mr / Mrs / Miss / Ms /(Dr)/ Other: .... Surname: ROBERTS............................
First Name: PAUL............................ Middle Name: ANTHONY............................
Maiden Name: n/a............
Date of Birth: 11/07/74............ Place of Birth: WOKING............... Nationality: BRITISH............
Passport No: 316885543............ Date of Issue: 01/03/06............ Date of Expiry: 01/03/16............
Passport issued by (Authority/Agency) UKPA......................
Occupation: DOCTOR............
Permanent Address: 26, HULL ROAD, CARDIFF............................ Postcode: BA7 9RR............

Reason for visit: TO VISIT FRIEND........................
Date of arrival: 15/09/200X Date of departure: 30/09/200X............

Date: .... Signature of Applicant ....

D

1 *Your own answer. Possible answer*:
We stayed at the Quality Rest Hotel in the centre of Oxford last week for two nights. It is superbly located very close to the city centre, but unfortunately there is no parking and you have to park in a very expensive public car park nearby. The room was comfortable and the decoration tasteful and contemporary. However, it was very small for a double-room and there was no bath, only a shower.

Also, there were two minor irritations. The remote control for the TV wasn't working and the hotel was incredibly slow to replace it; and internet access isn't free – you have to pay by the hour.

The evening restaurant is good and reasonably priced but the buffet breakfast was disappointing and lacking in imagination. All we had was some not very good coffee, toast, cheese and a yoghurt; there was no hot food or fruit.

All in all, not a bad hotel and quite good value for money, but I wouldn't recommend it to anyone with a car.

2 b bitterly c remarkably d particularly e fascinating
f disappointed

E

b 2 c 1 d 2 e 1 f 2 g 2 h 1 i 2 j 1

F

2 a SP b accommodation
3 a P b Vancouver
4 a VF or G b comes
5 a WO b Could you give me some idea
6 a SP b recommend
7 a V b journey/trip
8 a VF b hearing

Unit 7

Get ready to write

- a before: to remind themselves of the questions
  b during: as a record of what was said.
- An employee might leave a note to remind him/her to order something; to explain about a customer that phoned to complain.

A

1 2 D 3 C 4 E 5 A
2 b NB c a.m. d c.f. e etc.
3 b p.t. c wks d IT e asap
4 a to call you b see you c late
5 Your own answers. Possible answers:

A … two weeks in Poland and Hungary, preferably in three-star hotels if they are available, but two-star hotels are acceptable if necessary. They want to travel by train and definitely not by coach.

B … forgot to call you last night. I will be late for lectures this morning. Can you take notes? I'll see you as soon as possible.

C … very traditional. The steak and roast potatoes were very good. The vegetarian meals are satisfactory but there is very little choice. Overall, prices were reasonable.

D … ask the trainees personal questions about their experiences and if necessary talk about the basic equipment that is required (for example, a modem) and how it's used for email, the Internet and so on. Then the trainer will compare different software applications.

E … a good professional background and excellent IT skills. She is lively and enthusiastic; she would prefer to work part time, if possible.

Focus on abbreviations

b Sep / Sept c Dr 4 kph d admin. e ltd. f no. of opps

6 a It's extraordinary you've been a … for over … Is it true you've made …?
b Fit? – how many hrs a day exerc.?
c 40+ yrs; diff.; a.m.; frgn.
d 200 FILMS; EXERCISE; children
e 40 yrs. !!!!; over 200 films????
f + (= more than); % (= per cent); ∴ (because)
7 Your own answer. Possible answer:
1 Movie actor 40+ yrs.!!! – 200+ FILMS????
2 Diff. kp. fit when filmg? – Hrs. per day EXERCISE? – gym a.m. before set??? (unlikely)
3 Approx. 90% fans childr.? Why???!!! Strange ∴ always play fright. vllns.??? - eg frgn. agent ltst. BOND

Extra practice

1 Your own answer. Possible answer:
The customer's name; the problem; the dates; the order number.
2 Your own answer. Possible answer:
charged $150 – offer $99 on web – Rhea Gambhir – order 21st? 23rd? last mth.
– NO ORDER NO.! – tel. 0091 22 220 5516

Class bonus

Your own answers. Possible answers:
A Mrs Scarlatti (Leonardo Bus. Sch. – Italy) phoned. Wants 10+ work plcmnts. Oct. Aswr v. qckly!!!!
B comp. overhtng. after 2+ hrs – scr. freezes – rmvd cover → worked OK but damgd. sthg. !! HELP!!!!! (???)

Unit 8

Get ready to write

- a Explaining how to get somewhere or how to use a new piece of equipment
  b Good instructions use short phrases and simple language; they show, step by step, the order in which things are to be done; they are clear and easy to read; visual highlighting is used where possible.

A

1 a 2 b 3 c 1
2 a 3 b 2 c 1
3 b 1 omits punctuation; 2 uses ordinary punctuation and capital letters for highlighting; 3 uses ordinary punctuation without highlighting
c 1 uses indefinite articles and omits you; 2 omits all articles and you; 3 includes articles and often uses you
d 1 is simple, direct and impersonal. It uses numbers to show sequencing as in a list. It is neither polite nor impolite and appropriate to the context. 2 is slightly 'softer' and has a more polite 'feel' because it uses sequence words (First, etc.) instead of numbers, more words to explain things and the word 'please'. 3 is friendly, direct and polite and probably written to someone the writer knows.

Focus on clauses of time, condition and reason/purpose

Your own answers. Possible answers:
b After you've finished / you finish (having) dinner, give me a ring.
c If it's cold tonight, light a fire.
d In order to finish the report, you'll need to stay at work late.
e So that you don't get lost, please take a map.
f When you get up at 6.00 tomorrow, make me a cup of tea.

4 Your own answer. Possible answer:
SOCIAL ORGANIZER
Weekly activity sheet
MONDAY
Join with teachers to welcome new students.
Buy food and drink for evening reception.
TUESDAY
Go round classes and advertise this week's activities.
Plan the following week's activities.
Take students on guided walk round city.
WEDNESDAY
Check which students want evening activity in school (e.g. quiz)/which students want sports (e.g. tennis). Make sure staff available, courts booked, etc.

THURSDAY
Organize barbecue. Put up sign-up sheets for weekend excursion.
FRIDAY
Check names and numbers for excursion. Take deposits and phone tour company. Make sure tour guide available.
SATURDAY
Accompany students on excursion. Introduce students to tour guide.

5 *Your own answer. Possible answer:*

The first thing you do on Monday is join with the teachers and welcome the new students. Then you go out and buy some food and drink for the evening reception.

On Tuesday, you go round the classes and advertise the week's activities. After you've done that, you'll need to plan the following week's activities. Then after lessons, you take the students on a walk around the city.

On Wednesday, check which students want to take part in the evening activity in the school and which students prefer to do sports, such as tennis. If there are enough students for tennis, make sure that staff are available and that the courts are booked.

On Thursday, you'll need to organize the barbecue as well as put up sign-up sheets for the weekend excursion.

On Friday, check the names of the students going on the excursion, take their deposits, phone the tour company and make sure a tour guide is available.

Then on Saturday, accompany the students on their excursion and introduce them to the tour guide.

I hope all that's clear. Of course, I'll be here when you arrive to go through it all again and answer any questions you have.

B

3 a there is no emergency phone number, nothing about not re-entering the building and there is nothing about attacking the fire if possible.
   b Improving presentation: have bullet points or numbers for each point; highlight (e.g. underline) ALL the key phrases (not just one)
      Improving overall structure: it is more logical to put *Report to the assembly point* AFTER the instruction about belongings.
      Improving style: use imperatives; avoid contractions; sound less personal and colloquial

4 *Your own answer. Possible answer:*
FIRE INSTRUCTIONS

If you discover a fire
1 Sound the alarm
2 Phone the fire brigade (999)
3 Attack the fire if possible using the available appliances

If you hear the fire alarm
4 Leave the building immediately by the quickest route
5 Do not stop to collect personal belongings
6 Report to the assembly point

Do not re-enter the building until you are authorized to do so.

Unit 9

A

1 a 3 b 1 c 2
2 a True b False – Somebody wrote some notes after the meeting as a record of what Sarah said in her report c True
3 The writer's personal opinion is acceptable in 3.
4 1: number ; names ; abbreviations
   2: Key points ; Action ; little
   3: symbols ; punctuation ; topic ; a general conclusion
5 *Your own answer. Possible answer:*
A shorter working week?
In France, in 2000 the Government made the working week a maximum of 35 hours (averaged over the year).

PROS
It would lead to:
• higher employment; there would be more work for more people
• more leisure time
• the workers would be less tired

CONS
What often happened was
• there was not higher employment; neither employees nor employers wanted small part-time jobs
• there was more leisure time but in the private sector at least there was no more money to enjoy it so the workers were unhappy
• the workers were <u>more</u> tired because they were expected to work harder in fewer hours

SUMMARY
It could be seen as an interesting experiment.
6 *Your own answer. Possible answer:*
S&M : SW
* sales ↓3.4%
* mkt. *share China* ↓
* new *mkts. Russ.?*
Sales: mkt. *res. proj.*
7 a provide a reminder of what is agreed
   b you
   c as abbreviated notes that you will write up after the meeting
8 *Your own answer.*

Focus on spelling of plural nouns

b taxis c addresses d boxes e journeys f countries
g months h babies

---

9 *Your own answer. Possible answer*:
DATE/TIME
the last Wed. (ev.)
TYPE OF EVENT
buffet + drinks. Speech – Roberto? (prob.)
GUEST LIST
Pres. staff only + ptnrs.
VENUE
Main recep. area
FOOD
Outside ctrs.
WHO TO ORGANIZE
Ilya + ???(everyone else)

Extra practice

Your own answer. Possible answer:
LEAVING PARTY
Date/time
• The last Wednesday in the evening
Type of event
• Buffet with drinks. Roberto to make a speech (probably)
Guest list
• Present staff only with their partners
Venue
• Main reception area
Food
• Use outside caterers
Who to organize
• Ilya with the support of everyone else

B

1 *Your own answer. Possible answer*:
Mass tourism ruins the environment and exploits local workers.
2 MAIN HEADING: *Mass tourism*
SUBHEADING 1: ✓ or *Pros* or *Advantages*
SUBHEADING 2: ✗ or *Cons* or *Disadvantages*
CONCLUDING HEADING: *What Needs to be Done*
3 *Your own answer. Possible answer*:
MASS TOURISM
✓
Cheap flights → more people see more
Jobs/Money for locals (in some places main source of inc.)
More eco-tourism now/more young people try and integrate

✗
Too many tourists → big int. hotels → destroy environ./culture
Seasonal work/low incomes x job secur.
Main money goes abroad/foreign bosses
Most tourists don't respect culture/just want holiday

WHAT NEEDS TO BE DONE
Greater protect. for environ./wildlife/rights of local workers
Keep money in the country
Educate people in different cultures

Unit 10

Get ready to write

⊙ a in an airport
   b in a hotel
⊙ a when your luggage has been lost; your flight delayed or cancelled; overbooking so there are no more seats available
   b overbooking so there are no rooms available; no record of your booking; the facilities are not working/dirty; the attitude of staff

A

1 E, I, D, B, H, F, C, A, G
2 a
3 She wants the radios to be replaced.
4 subject line B
reference to previous contact H
name and title G
formal ending A
explanation of the problem F
address of person receiving the letter I
formal greeting D
the company sending the letter and the date it was written E
explanation of what is needed C
5 a (We) have been generally satisfied with the service you offer.
   b the last two deliveries have proved very unsatisfactory.
   c damaged on arrival
   d we have still not received replacements.
   e We trust that this situation does not indicate a decline in your service standards
6 Mrs Jamali is apologizing for not arranging for someone to meet the person at the airport.
7 Thanks for your note; I'm really sorry; I've checked it out; I'm sure you understand; I'm really sorry about the mix-up; that it won't stop you working with us!
8 Formal and polite.
9 Problem 1: Parking   Problem 2: Room location
Problem 3: State of rooms
10 *Your own answer. Possible answer*:
d, b, e, f, g, c, a

Focus on participle clauses

b Not having had any exercise all day, he felt like going for a walk.
c While hating the job, he couldn't afford to give it up.
d Being ill, Peter spent all day in bed.
e Since last seeing you, I got married.
f Having lived in Warsaw all her life, Klara knows the city very well.
g Turning right at the crossroads, the car went north.
h Having been directed by an artist, the film was very beautiful to look at.

11 *Your own answer. Possible answer*:

I'm writing to complain about the service we received at your hotel on Thursday 14th July.

As you will see from my fax of 30th June (attached), a group reservation was made for eight of our staff for one night, but in the event the booking was entirely unsatisfactory.

First of all, we had been promised three reserved car parking spaces. However, on arrival it turned out that there were none available and we had to park at a nearby public car park at considerable expense to the company.

Also, we had been promised adjoining rooms so that our team could work together and prepare for the conference they were attending. As it turned out, all of them were located on different floors and, to make matters worse, the lift was out of order.

Furthermore, there were considerable problems on arrival. The rooms were not ready when we arrived at 2 pm and two of our team said their rooms had not been properly cleaned. One said the air conditioning was not working in her room and another was put on a smoking corridor when we had requested non-smoking rooms.

On complaining at reception, my staff were told rather rudely that your hotel was short-staffed and that there was nothing that could be done about it.

Considering the number of years we have used your hotel and generally been satisfied with your service, we trust that this situation was untypical. However, in the circumstances I must insist on a complete refund.

B

1   There were two managers, not three.
    It was a Human Resources workshop, not a Communications workshop.
    Did not receive an email confirmation.
    No deposit was asked for or accepted.
    It wasn't the second time this has happened, it was the first.

3   *Your own answer. Possible answer:*
    Dear Rick

    Thanks for giving me a call about the Human Resources workshop. Yes, I'd heard that there had been a bit of a problem and that two of your team were turned away.

    The problem was that we could only accept 25 people on the workshop and we had over 50 applications. Your office only got in touch after we had closed applications. I don't know who it was you spoke to in the first place but they should never have said there were spaces. I'll certainly look into it and make sure it never happens again. I'm really very sorry – as you say, you've been good clients of ours for a long time and there have never been any problems.

    Anyway, what I can say is we've decided to run a similar workshop next month. If you're still interested I'll make sure your names are at the top of the list, and as a way of saying sorry, I'm happy to offer a 50% discount on the fee. I hope that's acceptable.

    Let me know if you're interested.

Unit 11

Get ready to write

○   *Your own answers.*
○   *Your own answers.*
○   *Your own answers.*

A

1   They are probably businessmen.
2   a are not   b are not   c politely
3   b 3   c 1
4   1 *Would it be possible*   2 *If you would… I could….*
    3 *It would be very helpful if…*
5   1 I'm visiting   2 you will be coming   3 I'm arriving
6   *Your own answers.*
7   You do not want him to meet you at the airport, discuss the programme in the car and then go to the company. You want to go to the hotel and check in.
8   *Your own answers. Possible answers:*
    Paragraph 2 Plans on arrival
    Paragraph 3 Plans for the next morning
    Paragraph 4 Plans for the afternoon
    Paragraph 5 Departure plans
9   *Your own answers.*

Focus on talking about future travel plans

a   I'm visiting (it is a personal arrangement already made, not a public programme); I'll be staying (it is something already arranged for the whole period)
b   I'm staying (personal arrangement)
c   you're going to do (your intentions are)
d   opens (a fixed public regular event; *going to* would suggest a special planned event or intention)
e   due to arrive (it is expected at a certain time)
f   I'm going to arrive (the speaker is making a prediction about being late; *I'm arriving* would suggest a personal arrangement)
g   bound to be (which means 'certain' – it always is full; *likely* means probable, which is weaker)

---

10 *Your own answer. Possible answer:*
    Thank you very much for your kind offer to meet me from my flight on the 4th, which as you say, arrives in Moscow at 4.30 in the afternoon. My assistant has already booked me a taxi to take me to my hotel, which saves you the trouble of having to fight your way through the traffic at that time of day. Also I think I would like to check into the hotel first after such a long flight.

11 *Your own answer. Possible answer:*
    Dear Mr Zhirkov

    Thank you very much for your kind offer to meet me from my flight on the 4th, which as you say, arrives in Moscow at 4.30 in the afternoon. My assistant has already booked me a taxi to take me to my hotel, which saves you the trouble of having to fight your way through the traffic at that time of day. Also, I think I would like to check into the hotel first after such a long flight.

    Rather than come to the company on Monday evening, can I suggest we meet for dinner in the evening at my hotel, say at 7.30? If I'm not there it means I've been held up somewhere, in which case I'll try and get a message through to you. Could you email me the number of your mobile?

    The next morning before coming to Capital I have an appointment with the General Manager of Alma Bank, which is very close by, I believe. My plan is to be with you by 11.00. Could you possibly meet me at reception and give me a tour of the company?

    I think we agreed that before we start our discussions at 2.00, I'd have lunch with your staff in the cafeteria. Is that still OK?

My plane home leaves at 8.05, but, don't worry, I'll arrange for a taxi when I'm there.

Really looking forward to meeting you again.

B

3 *Your own answer. Possible answer*:
10-DAY CULTURE AND HISTORY TOUR OF FRANCE

March 1st

am

Eurostar London–Paris
Depart *7.09 London*
Arrive *Paris 10.59 (local time)*
Coach to *hostel (Boissière)*

pm

Guided coach tour of Paris (e.g. Eiffel Tower, Notre Dame)

March 2nd–5th

am

Classes on French culture and history (TBA)

pm

Afternoon visits to art galleries, places of historical interest (e.g. Louvre, Versailles)

March 6th

am

TGV *to Avignon*
Coach *to hotel (TBA)*

pm

Visit to palace/bridge.

March 7th–8th

Coach tour of *South of France* (e.g. *countryside, coast, historical sites, museums, art galleries, gardens*) (TBA)

March 9th

Day trip to Monaco.
(Selected lectures at *International University*)

March 10th

Coach to Nice airport.
Return to the UK

4 *Your own answer. Possible answer*:

I've spoken to the French travel agent and agreed on a rough outline for the tour.

We'll get the Eurostar on the 1st at 7.09. This gets in at 10.59 local time. After that we'll be taken by coach to our hostel and in the afternoon have a coach tour of Paris.

Then, as you know, for the next four days we're having morning classes on French culture and history, followed by visits in the afternoon to art galleries. However, the agent hasn't yet fixed up the classes yet.

Then on the 6th we'll get the TGV to Avignon and have a tour of the palace and bridge in the afternoon.

On the 7th and 8th the plan is to have a coach tour of the South of France but nothing's been arranged so far.

On the 9th, we'll have a day trip to Monaco, which will include some lectures at the International University, and then on the 10th we'll get the coach to Nice airport and return to the UK.

Hope all that's clear.

Unit 12

Get ready to write
- *Your own answers.*
- One advantage for the student: they get practical experience of working in a real company.
- One advantage for the company: lower labour costs.

A

1 a A company is considering offering internships to students and recent graduates and wants to research the advantages and disadvantages.
  b The readers will probably be the managers involved in making the decision.

2 2 INTRODUCTION 3 MAIN SECTION 4 CONCLUSION

3 b Introduction c Conclusion and recommendation
  d Introduction e Disadvantages

4 numbers; headings

5 clear and neutral; balanced

6 b 3 c 5 d 2 e 1

7 in the main: 4 (This report) is intended to: 1 all things considered: 3 the majority (of staff) felt that: 2 we have no hesitation in proposing: 5 there is little doubt that: 3

9 set up a committee/seek external funding

10 *Current facilities* because that is what you have been asked to survey; and then maybe *Strengths and limitations* because you are contrasting what is good with what is weak.

11 b. (a is logical but the headings are not right; c is logical but the headings are not general enough)

Focus on writing in a neutral style

1 *Your own answers. Possible answers*:
  b In order to prepare for/As preparation for this report, I interviewed a cross-section of students and staff.
  c At present/At the present time/Currently
  d While the people I interviewed liked the gym and appreciated the facilities there, most felt that the other sports facilities were totally inadequate.
  e In my view/opinion the committee should …
2 set up; report; make; suggest; raising; are needed

---

13 *Your own answer. Possible answer*:
REPORT ON COLLEGE SPORTS FACILITIES
Introduction
The main aims of this report are to
1 give an overview of the sports facilities in the college
2 comment on whether the facilities meet the needs of students and staff
3 recommend a way forward.

As preparation for this report, I interviewed a cross-section of students and staff.

Current facilities
At present, the college has a 15-metre swimming pool, a small sports hall used for netball and volleyball, a large gym with over 100 fitness stations and three tennis courts. There are a number of sports clubs and societies, most of which use off-site facilities.

Strengths and limitations

While the people I interviewed liked the gym and appreciated the facilities there, most students and staff felt that the other sports facilities were totally inadequate. They said

- the swimming pool was much too small
- the sports hall was also too small and unable to accommodate badminton, five-a-side football etc.
- there were too few tennis courts and they were in a bad state of repair.

Most people I spoke to felt that major investment in new facilities was required.

Recommendations

In my view, a sports committee, consisting of students and staff, should be set up to draw up a plan for future developments and report to the Principal. This committee should:

- make realistic proposals for improvements over the next 5 years
- suggest methods of raising the funds needed.

B

1 a Air pollution, water shortage and too many tourists
  b Slightly improved air quality; better piping for water; a new eco-tourism programme which wants tourists to respect the environment
  c No
2 a Yes b Yes c No d No. Sometimes it is too personal
  e No f *Your own answers.*
3 *Your own answer. Possible answer:*

REPORT ON MAIN CURRENT ENVIRONMENTAL ISSUES FACING OUR COUNTRY

Introduction

In recent years, our country's economy has grown rapidly. However, because we have failed to protect the environment adequately there are significant environmental problems.

Main problem areas

1 Air pollution
   Air pollution is a serious problem in all the major cities of our country, mainly as a result of exhaust fumes from ageing vehicles. It is a major cause of disease and respiratory difficulties.
2 Water
   The average citizen in our country uses 300 litres of water a day, and with recent dramatic increases in the population far more water is being taken from the ground than can be replaced by rainfall.
3 Tourism
   Because of the number of tourists now visiting our country sites of natural beauty are gradually being destroyed.

Successes

1 Recent controls on vehicles have slightly improved air quality.
2 The water companies are replacing pipes to reduce the number of water leaks.
3 The government has launched an eco-tourism programme which aims to get tourists to respect the environment.

Conclusion and recommendations

Despite the successes, far more still needs to be done in all three areas. The environment is being damaged and far more needs to be done if we are to protect human health and life in general.

Unit 13

Get ready to write
○ a Monet b Renoir c Pissarro
○ *Your own answers.*

A

2 b 1 (to suggest atmosphere rather than showing exact details)
  c 1 (that uses colour to show the effects of light);
     3 (Changes in natural light are emphasized… reflection of colours from object to object)
  d 3 (Colours…with as little mixing as possible)
  e 2 (by painting outdoors)
3 a relevant b this style of painting also influenced painters in the United States
4 *Your own answers.*
5 *Your own answers.*
6 2 F 3 T 4 F 5 F 6 T 7 T 8 T 9 F

> **Focus on defining relative clauses**
>
> b which/that c whose d when e who f where
> g who h which/that

7 *Your own answer. Possible answer:*
We have been thrilled by horror films, films in which very frightening, unnatural things happen, since films were first made. They allow us to be frightened without actually being in danger.

In the early 1930s there were many successful American Gothic horror films and ones which mix in science fiction and more serious German expressionist films of the 1920s. However, in the 1950s low-budget American horror films were more science fiction (for example, alien invasions) while the British made more bloody Technicolor films with classic horror characters like Dracula.

Since then two films which best illustrate the genre are *Psycho* (1960) and *The Blair Witch Project* (1999). Most critics agree that *Psycho* is a complex psychological thriller, although one critic has described it as 'a tremendously successful confidence trick'. It is about a woman who, having stolen some money, is on the run when she pulls into a lonely motel and there is an horrific murder. *The Blair Witch Project* is about three film students who go into the woods to make a film about a local legend and never return. According to one critic, it is an 'extraordinarily effective horror film' because it has 'no fancy special effects'.

Extra practice

3   *Your own answer. Possible answer:*
Both Dr Martin Luther King, Jr (1929–68) and Nelson Mandela (1918–) are best-known as powerful black leaders who championed the civil rights of blacks – in King's words 'to equip him to compete on a just and equal basis'. As a result of their struggle, both received the Nobel Peace Prize. However, while Martin Luther King was a minister for a Christian church, who used passive resistance to challenge the segregationist laws of the American South, Nelson Mandela was a lawyer who joined the armed struggle of the African National Congress (ANC). Mandela was arrested and sent to prison, where he stayed for 27 years, but King was shot dead by a white assassin. Whereas King's death led to riots in dozens of towns in the US, when Mandela was released crowds danced in the streets. After Mandela's release he was involved in negotiations which led to South Africa's first all-race elections, became President of South Africa and is now a retired elder statesman.

Unit 14

Get ready to write

○   *Your own answers.*
○   *Your own answer.*

A

1   b 4   c 1   d 3
2   1 a   2 b   3 a   4 b
3   a   unlikely situation + result: Extract 3. The second conditional (*if* + past + *would/could/might* + infinitive) is used because the writer doesn't really think it is very likely that we will use bicycles more often and reduce pollution. It is an imaginary situation about the present and future.
possible situation + result: Extract 1. The writer uses a 'zero' conditional (*if* + present + present/*can*). Not eating meat and losing balance in our diet are possible everyday situations and the writer is giving the result of what happens in these situations.
   b   Extract 2: … *they love **it*** (= sport) … *see **their*** (= professionals') *sport… out of **it*** (= sport) *as… than **it*** (= amateur sport being part of the community) *is in professional sport*
   c   Extract 4: … *that **they*** (= many normal, stable people) *are not in a situation where **they*** (= normal stable, people) … *and if **they*** (= normal, stable people) *do… want to get to know **them*** (= new people) … *before we actually meet **them*** (= new people)

Focus on avoiding repetition

b   these/such   c   one   d   their   e   them
f   the former … the latter / (the) one … the other

---

4   a   Probably to make a comparison and give your opinions.
   b   You can either make a comparison between alternatives within the same paragraphs as you go along or give all the arguments 'for' and then all the arguments 'against' in separate paragraphs.
   c   It's not an article for a magazine so your style will be clear, balanced and neutral.
   d   If you have presented both sides of the argument clearly and fairly, and given your own opinion; if you have used accurately and appropriately some standard phrases often used in compositions.

5–8   *Your own answers.*
   9   b 2   c 1   d 4
11   *Your own answer. Possible answer:*
Is working for yourself really much better than working for someone else? These days, with improved technology, more people are working independently and while there are many advantages, it is not without its difficulties.

The main advantage of working for yourself is that you have the freedom to make choices about what you do and when you work. It's usually very flexible. There is nobody telling you what to do and when to do it. So, for example, if you want to take your family out for the day then that is up to you. Also, another big advantage, particularly if you work from home, is that you have more time to work since you don't have to spend hours on the train going to and from the office and you can work in the evenings or weekends if you want.

On the other hand, working for yourself gives you lots of worries. You don't have the security you get from working for someone else. For example, you don't get sick pay and you have little legal protection. Also, while you have flexibility not to work, there is always the temptation to work during time your family would expect you to be with them.

On balance though, working for yourself can give you a lot more job satisfaction than working for someone else, but you have to be very disciplined and organize your time carefully.

Extra practice

4   *Your own answer. Possible answer:*
It depends what you want: holidays on the beach or holidays in the city.
Holidays are important for all of us. Whether we decide to have a city holiday or a holiday by the beach depends upon our personal preferences. The main thing is we are taking a break from our usual routine.

Of course, the main difference between city holidays and beach holidays is in the kind of activities you are able to do. At the beach, for example, you can swim, go sailing, water-ski or surf. On the other hand, in a city you can go shopping, look at important buildings, visit museums or go to the theatre.

Another major difference is that having a holiday by the beach tends to be more relaxing. When you're in a city you spend all your time getting on buses, getting into taxis, walking, visiting museums, going to the cinema. Although this can be very exciting you have to organize what you do very carefully and you can quickly get exhausted. The beach on the other hand is where time goes by more slowly. If you like, you can swim, lie in the sun or the shade, have a quiet drink and go to sleep. The pace of life is a lot slower and doesn't require as much energy!

Although perhaps it's not such an important difference, nevertheless you have to think about the clothing and equipment you are going to take, depending on the kind of holiday it is. If you are going to the beach you can travel light with bathing suit, shorts and sandals, but in the city you will need clothes for walking, such as jeans and trainers, and smarter clothes in case you want to go to a play or a concert.

All in all, I usually prefer beach holidays because they are more relaxing, but sometimes I like the excitement of going to a famous city and looking at the sights. It all depends on what mood I'm in and how hard I've been working.

Unit 15

A

1 b 1 c 2

2 B 2 C 1

3 a B: This table gives … C: This chart tells us … (These phrases are used to introduce what the chart/table/graph shows.)

  b The present perfect is used because the populations are described from a point in the past (1950) and the growth is still continuing now. Note that the past simple is used when a specific (and finished) point in the past is being described (*In 1950… Mexico City… **had***).

  c Because it is written in the present (*are happy*); if they had left it would have been written in the past.

  d Because it is not important who actually did these things, like spend the money on rent. These are averages anyway.

  e Because the focus is only on the main information and trends.

> **Focus on analyzing trends**
>
> 1 b *fell slightly* c *sharp drop*
>   d *significant improvement* e *upwards*
>   f *were at their lowest*
> 2 b *of* c *in* d *With*

4 a Largest: 15- to 64-year olds; Smallest: 65 and over

  b That there are quite a lot more women than men.

  c There are slightly more males than females.

5 *Your own answers. Possible answers*:

  Perhaps only two paragraphs, one for each chart. You can combine the information for the 0–14 and 15–64 age groups. Since you are describing a present situation, you will use present verb forms.

> **Focus on comparing information**
>
> b Much the smallest c more women than men
> d boys as girls e the best statistics
> f are more meaningful than those
> g The older the age group, the greater the gender difference.

6 *Your own answer. Possible answer*:

  The pie chart at the top shows/highlights clearly that the largest age group (69%) is between 15 and 64, with a small percentage (18%) aged 0–14. The smallest age group is the over-65s (13%).

  However, the bar chart below it shows that while there are more or less the same number of men and women between the ages of 0 and 64 (approximately 14 million of each gender) there are about a third more women than men aged over 65 (2.5 million as opposed to 1.8 million).

Unit 16

A

1, 2 and 3 *Your own answers.*

> **Focus on quotations**
>
> b more exclusive'. (Be consistent: either use double quotation marks (") or single quotation marks (') around one quotation.)
> c luxury'. (Don't forget the full stop.)
> d 1950: 'Club Med started as an idealistic village.' (Use a colon, not a semi-colon and put the full stop before the quotation mark.)
> e says, 'each resort would provide … services and activities in one single package'. (Don't forget the comma, use only three dots to show that the words are missing and use only one full stop.)

4 *Your own answers. Possible answers*:
  a The smashing of plates.
  b Because it can be dangerous for other customers.

c   The throwing of flowers.

d   In different ways, e.g. it is linked to high spirits and fun; it keeps away evil spirits; it can symbolize good luck and a happy, lasting marriage; it can relieve worries; it can show appreciation of music and dancing.

e   Yes, at family parties held every three months.

5–7 *Your own answers.*

Focus on sentence combining

b   To make it less dangerous, some restaurateurs have replaced plates with flowers.
Since it is less dangerous, some restaurateurs have replaced plates with flowers.

c   Despite the fact that there are many risks,/Despite the many risks, some restaurateurs still allow plate smashing.
There are many risks but some restaurateurs still allow plate smashing.

d   Wanting to continue the tradition of plate smashing, some restaurateurs will still allow it.
Some restaurateurs will still allow plate smashing because they want to continue the tradition.

---

8 *Your own answer. Possible answer*:
The tradition of smashing plates at Greek restaurants is disappearing in the UK because owners fear they will be sued by customers hit by flying crockery. Some restaurateurs have replaced plates with flowers because it is less dangerous. Over the years the tradition has been interpreted in different ways: it is linked to high spirits and fun, it keeps away evil spirits, it can symbolize good luck and a happy, lasting marriage, it can relieve your worries and it can show appreciation of the music or dancing. Despite the many risks, some restaurateurs insist that they will continue the tradition for their family parties.

Extra practice

2 *Your own answer. Possible answer*:
Japanese business etiquette is quite different from that of many other countries and learning some local etiquette is very important.

Appearance
Both businessmen and businesswomen should dress conservatively.
Business entertaining
Business entertaining usually takes place in restaurants or bars after business hours. However, an invitation to get together socially 'might just be polite talk' rather than genuine.

Gift-giving
It is customary to give a small carefully-wrapped gift with both hands at the end of your visit.

Business cards
Business cards are very important and should be treated respectfully.

Physical gestures
Another point to remember is not to make any physical gestures which draw attention to yourself but you might want to make notes, which is a sign of respect.
However, despite these 'rules', Japanese people will understand if we make any unintended mistakes in etiquette.

Review2

A

Your own answers. Possible answers:
b i.e.   c kph   d dpt   e no.   f ✓   g c.f.   h ∴   i e.g.
j =   k etc.   l MD

B

Your own answer. Possible answer:
Some research published this week shows that you don't have to be rich to be happy. On the list of the world's happiest nations the richest countries come near the bottom and the tiny Pacific island of Vanuatu comes top.

C

b provided by your company   c I have had nothing but problems
d First of all   e your technician to arrive   f very unhelpful
g Eventually   h On top of that   i Furthermore   j dissatisfied

D

Your own answer. Possible answer:
VENETIAN RICE AND BEAN SOUP
300 g long-grain rice
200 g dried beans
½ l of beef stock
½ onion (chopped)
50 g butter
50 g smoked bacon (diced)
3 tablespoons olive oil
Salt and pepper

1   First, wash the beans, leave to soak for at least 12 hours, then drain.
2   Heat the oil and butter in saucepan and sauté the onion and bacon.
3   After a few minutes, add the beans, cover with plenty of water and bring to the boil.
4   Put a lid on and cook on a moderate heat for two hours.
5   Pour in stock and add rice and leave till rice is cooked.
6   Add salt and pepper to taste.

E

Your own answer. Possible answer:
Guy Richard's Plenary on *Recent Developments in Climate Change* opened the conference and his main conclusions were that
1   climate change *was partly caused by greenhouse gases*
2   global temperatures *are likely to rise between 1.4 and 5.8 °C this century*
3   *the risks were more serious than had previously been thought.*

F

Your own answer. Possible answer:
Monday: Arrive Port Elizabeth Airport. Collect hire car and drive to Park Inn Hotel.
Tuesday: Drive 100 km to St Francis Bay. Check into Oasis Lodge Hotel.
Wednesday: Optional activities: walking, golf, fishing or watersports.
Thursday: Day tour of lion park and elephant park. Dinner in hotel.
Friday: Day visit to game farm. Options: driving, horseriding or cycling.

Answer key

G

b significant   c purchases   d included   e convenience
f savings   g although   h disappointed

H

b interesting   c effects   d one's   e worst   f that   g find
h their   i facilities   j used   k to have   l appreciate
m Secondly   n responsible   o want   p achieve
q is going to clean   r clothes

I

b I've applied for a job with an export company, about which I know
   nothing.
c Not having eaten for 24 hours, I felt very hungry.
d Since you haven't been to class for the last two weeks, I'm going
   to write to your parents.
e I'll post the letter today to make sure it gets there for your
   brother's birthday.
f While knowing that we couldn't afford the rent, we decided to
   take the flat.
g After entering/After I entered the room, I realized something was
   wrong.
h Having been attacked by Tania's dog, I didn't want to go round to
   her house again.
i Marco wore a raincoat so that he wouldn't/didn't get wet.
j What was your reaction on seeing your old friend?